Signature SELF-TALK

Master the Art of Influencing *Yourself*

MELISSA HOLY

Copyright © 2023 by Melissa Holy

All rights reserved. Printed in the United States of America. No part of this publication or its associated ancillary materials may be reproduced, stored in a retrieval system or transmitted in any form or by any means, electronic, mechanical, photocopying, recording or otherwise, without the written permission of the publisher.

Published by: BridgeLight Publishing, Oak Hills, California
contact@bridgelightpublishing.com

Signature Self-Talk
ISBN 979-8-9881452-1-9 (Hardcover); ISBN 979-8-9881452-0-2 (eBook)

Library of Congress Control Number: 2023906881

DISCLAIMER AND LIMIT OF LIABILITY: The author and publisher make no representations or warranties with respect to the accuracy or completeness of the contents of this book. Although the teachings, practices, disciplines, techniques, and examples in this book are intended to be useful, it is sold with the understanding that this book and its associated ancillary materials, including verbal and written training, is not intended for use as a source of legal, investment, accounting, psychological, emotional, health, medical or other professional advice or services. The author and publisher specifically disclaim any implied warranties of merchantability or fitness for a particular purpose. Consult with a qualified professional when appropriate. The author and publisher specifically disclaim any liability, loss, or risk incurred as a consequence, directly or indirectly, of the use and application of any of the contents of this work. Neither the author nor the publisher shall, under any circumstances, be held liable to any party (or third party) for any damages, including but not limited to direct, indirect, punitive, special, incidental or other consequential damages, including any financial loss, commercial, personal, or other damages, arising directly or indirectly from any use of this book and related materials and or trainings, which are provided "as is" and without warranties.
EARNINGS & INCOME DISCLAIMER: This book and all related products and services are for educational and informational purposes only. The author and publisher make no warranties, guarantees,

representations, or claims of any kind. Reader's results will vary depending on a number of factors. The author and publisher are not responsible for the success or failure or your personal, business, health, or financial decisions relating to any information presented by the author or publisher, or any related products/services. No representation in any part of this information, materials, or training are guarantees or promises for actual performance. Results are entirely dependent on the efforts, skills, and application of the individual person.

Scripture quotations taken from the Amplified® Bible (AMP), Copyright © 2015 by The Lockman Foundation. Used by permission. www.Lockman.org. Scriptures and additional materials quoted and marked (GNT) are from the Good News Bible © 1994 published by the Bible Societies/HarperCollins Publishers Ltd UK, Good News Bible© American Bible Society 1966, 1971, 1976, 1992. Used with permission. Scripture quotations marked (NASB®) taken from the New American Standard Bible®, Copyright © 1960, 1962, 1963, 1968, 1971, 1972, 1973, 1975, 1977, 1995 by The Lockman Foundation. Used by permission. All rights reserved. www.Lockman.org. Scripture quotations marked (NIV) are taken from the Holy Bible, New International Version®, NIV®. Copyright © 1973, 1978, 1984, 2011 by Biblica, Inc.™ Used by permission of Zondervan. All rights reserved worldwide, www.zondervan.com. The "NIV" and "New International Version" are trademarks registered in the United States Patent and Trademark office by Biblica, Inc.™ Scripture marked (NKJV) taken from the New King James Version®. Copyright © 1982 by Thomas Nelson. Used by permission. All rights reserved. Scripture quotations marked (NLT) are taken from the Holy Bible, New Living Translation, copyright ©1996, 2004, 2007, 2013 by Tyndale House Foundation. Used by permission of Tyndale House Publishers, Inc., Carol Stream, Illinois 60188. All rights reserved. Scripture quotations marked (TLB) are taken from The Living Bible copyright © 1971. Used by permission of Tyndale House Publishers, Inc., Carol Stream, Illinois 60188. All rights reserved. Scripture quotations marked TPT are from The Passion Translation®. Copyright © 2017, 2018 by Passion & Fire Ministries, Inc. Used by permission. All rights reserved. ThePassionTranslation.com. Italics in scriptures reflect the author's emphasis.

For information on special quantity book sales please email: contact@bridgelightpublishing.com

Dedication

First and foremost, I dedicate this book to my Lord and Savior, Jesus Christ, who empowers me to influence myself every day in a positive way.

To my incredible son, Colton, whose endless support and encouragement drive me to *never* give up on reaching for my dreams.

To my beautiful mom, Jackie, who consistently modeled the life of a strong woman of faith.

Table of Contents

INTRODUCTION: YOUR INNER WORLD 1

CHAPTER 1: THE STORM 5

CHAPTER 2: BUILDING A SOLID FOUNDATION 21

CHAPTER 3: WHY SELF-TALK MATTERS..39

CHAPTER 4: INFLUENCING YOURSELF 57

CHAPTER 5: ENCOURAGING YOURSELF 75

CHAPTER 6: PREPARING FOR TRANSFORMATION 93

CHAPTER 7: DISCOVERING YOUR SIGNATURE SOUND...........111

CHAPTER 8: CREATING YOUR SIGNATURE SYSTEM 127

CHAPTER 9: OPTIONS, ROUTINES, AND APPLICATIONS 145

CHAPTER 10: TRUE SUCCESS AND A LASTING LEGACY 165

CONCLUSION: THE SELF-TALK DARE 175

NOTES..179

Introduction

YOUR INNER WORLD

Since the day you were born, you've been communicating with yourself in one way or another. Whether inside, with your thoughts, or outside, with your voice. You say positive things, and you say negative things. You laugh at yourself, and you cry with yourself. You leave scribbled notes to keep yourself on track. You have a whole *inner* world happening that eventually shows up in everything you do in life on the *outside*. In short, no matter what is happening in the world, *your* world starts inside *you*.

Like a fuzzy picture coming into focus, this book will sharpen your awareness of how much your self-talk determines the quality of your life. It influences every one of your habits, your ambitions, and ultimately your destiny. With the simple strategies this book offers, you can put the powerhouse of your mind to work to masterfully turn your self-talk into your greatest asset and strongest ally. Dare yourself to stir up and use all God has given you to create and live your best life, no matter what is happening around you.

Suppose you could maximize every part of your life. How different would your levels of confidence, happiness, fitness, income, and achievement look than they do right now? Your self-talk is ground zero—the most critical area you can refine to trigger incredible progress and lasting change. You can set yourself up to win and succeed at the highest levels by developing what I call "signature self-talk." No matter how many voices speak into your life daily, God designed *your* voice to hold the *ultimate* influence over your life. Signature self-talk allows you to harness the power of that influence and leverage it to transform any area in your life you want to strengthen or change. As you discover how your signature voice can become an incredible tool for transformation and cultivate your *personalized* signature self-talk, you can shape your thoughts, speak powerfully into your own life, and influence yourself into action. It's time to use your self-talk for maximum advantage and master the art of influencing *yourself*!

Think of your self-talk as that monumental *first* domino that sets off a subsequent chain reaction in every detail of your life. It is the make-or-break factor in your health and happiness, faith and spiritual life, work and achievements, and overall success. Developing your signature self-talk is one of the most important investments you could ever make in yourself and your future. Using customized self-talk as a phenomenal *offensive tactic* can take your self-influence to a new level to produce the results you want in life. Changing how you show up for *yourself* will change how you show up in the world.

Through inspiring stories and the life-changing principles shared on these pages, you will learn how to elevate your inner game and be equipped and encouraged to make your best voice heard. Imagine being the most persuasive influencer for positive change in your own life. With an arsenal of personal, practical, profound messaging to help you stay attentive to your thought life, you can keep yourself *consistently* moving toward your goals. Whatever mission, vision, or challenge you face in your life, career, business, ministry, or leadership, be assured that you can design a brilliant signature message to help you reach your goal faster. The specialized self-talk you configure is *your* masterpiece to build.

Signature self-talk opens up new ways of thinking and problem-solving as you learn to reframe how you view self-control, habits and performance, motivation, mindfulness, stress, anxiety, and more. You will gain new tools to develop regular positive self-talk that will update your beliefs about yourself.

What makes this book different from other books on self-talk? I aspire to present a more personal, simplistic, and creative approach to the way we influence ourselves. I reveal valuable lessons from my journey, the life-changing strategies I've discovered, and my 4-step DARE System—all from a faith-based perspective. These pages will give you workable tools and actionable steps to equip you far beyond simply correcting negative thoughts. You will have a straightforward process and easy-to-apply techniques that will help to prevent wayward thinking before it even begins. Building your empowering signature self-talk *system* will allow you to sharpen self-awareness, shape day-to-day behaviors, drive personal development, improve health and habits, boost productivity, increase wealth, build new skills, retain information, multiply your impact, and more.

To gain the most value from this book, I recommend you read the chapters in order rather than skip around.

Your signature self-talk can have a higher impact when you fully understand how and why it works so well. You will find that each chapter progressively builds on the next, connecting all aspects of the system to one another in a clear and simple fashion. More than anything, I know that you want RESULTS. And that's what I want for you too. Incredible, life-changing, *lasting* results!

Signature self-talk is intended to help you strengthen and grow who you are *behind closed doors*, where you might struggle the most. When times are challenging, this book will give you solid tools that will equip you to face life courageously and with perseverance. Now is the time to step into and conquer new territory and to be spiritually, mentally, and emotionally *fit*, able to handle whatever happens in your life and the world. When you understand how to be deliberate in influencing your thinking and behavior, you can stand firm in faith and keep generating positive momentum in every area of your life.

Lastly, before we officially dive in, I invite you to visit SignatureSelfTalk.com for resources to help you enjoy and benefit from every part of this life-altering journey. Don't wait to get started. You have nothing to lose and everything to gain as you take hold of creating the best version of yourself and your extraordinary life ahead. Get ready for a great revival inside as you dare to revolutionize the way you talk to, influence, and encourage *yourself*.

Chapter 1

THE STORM

Jolted awake by the blaring house alarm at three o'clock in the morning, I jumped out of bed and scrambled to turn on a light. My heart pounding, I reached for my loaded handgun and quickly positioned myself in a corner behind the bed. Whispering a silent prayer, I could hardly believe this was happening. It seemed like a terrible nightmare, yet the danger felt very real. I feared what might come crashing through my bedroom door any minute.

Gun in hand, I stood frozen, trying to contain my chaotic thoughts. Who is in my house? *Where* are they? The piercing alarm was deafening and made it difficult to detect any motion downstairs. Unhinged thoughts of possible violence, even death, flashed through my mind. All I could do was stand there, numb, alone, and afraid. As the shrieking sound of the alarm pounded on, I waited.

It seemed like a lifetime before the phone finally rang with the alarm monitoring service responding to offer help. I quickly explained my situation as my heart beat wildly. The woman heard the urgency in my voice and assured me that the police would be on the way. I had hoped she would stay on the phone with me, but she unexpectedly disconnected the call, and the line went dead. Feeling alone again, I shifted my focus back to the raging threat in front of me. Barely blinking, I swallowed hard and stood braced and ready to shoot at the first sign of anyone approaching that bedroom door.

As I paused to take a deep breath, I became aware of a sudden strange sensation. Like a surge of strength and energy, I felt a rush of the presence and power of God fill me, and a wave of courage washed over me. Inexplicably, it began to overshadow and calm every frantic thought stirring my fear and confusion. My entire posture straightened, and I stood up taller. Before I knew it, powerful scriptures and declarations began pouring out of my mouth. My voice grew stronger and louder. A sense of control and authority took command of my thinking. Boldly I yelled toward the door at whoever *dared* to come near it! Everything inside me ignited, and I felt ready spiritually, mentally, emotionally, and even physically for whatever was going to happen.

The sound of the doorbell abruptly interrupted my shouting at my invisible enemy. Knowing the police had finally arrived, I tightened my grip on the revolver as I stepped toward the bedroom door. As I took another deep breath, I turned the knob and swung the door open, fully prepared to shoot if necessary. Step by step, I carefully made my way down the stairway. As I reached the entryway, I lowered my weapon and opened the front door. As I invited the officer inside, I described what had been happening. We walked around and thoroughly inspected every room in the house, yet we found nothing. After securing the entire property, I felt relieved and grateful.

But at the same time, I was still left wondering what could have set off the alarm.

As I crawled back into bed after the ordeal, my mind circled back to one scene in the dramatic sequence of events. I was stunned at what arose in me during those highly charged moments. I recalled the electrifying power I felt in my body and retraced what came streaming out of my mouth. Much more than an adrenaline rush, deep things surfaced in me under that extreme pressure. Not only was it an image of myself I would never forget, but I also felt that I would never be the same again after that startling experience.

"You can't tell the strong house without the storm."
—Charles Stanley

In the morning, I was determined to dig deeper for an explanation of what happened with the alarm system. With little detail, the monitoring service deemed it a false alarm. The dispatch center could only speculate that there must have been something faulty that triggered the motion detector. But it made no sense. Even more peculiar was that the motion detector was in a closed, quiet, and rarely used room.

Everyone I spoke with about the occurrence seemed baffled that the single motion device did not simply go offline or send an error code, as it typically would. Instead, for some unknown reason, it set off the entire house alarm system right in the middle of the night! Even today it remains a complete mystery as to why or how the malfunction occurred. It had never happened before, and it has never happened since. It was a traumatic and isolated event that would remain etched in my memory for a long time. But even more, it would turn out to be a night that God revealed something important to me, *about* me.

> **"Awake, awake! Put on your strength."**
> **—Isaiah 52:1 NKJV**

WHEN THE PRESSURE IS ON
What do we get when we squeeze an orange? Orange juice, of course. Well, that same logic can apply to us. When high pressure squeezes us, what's inside comes barreling out! One of the most revealing lessons we can learn about ourselves is finding out *exactly* what comes out of us when we face a fiery test.

That scary alarm incident was a high-pressure squeeze for me. But I believe God had a great purpose in allowing it to happen. I was able to witness firsthand what came out of me. I had the opportunity to watch myself in action. I got to see what I had in me. Completely alone, I believed I was in a life-threatening emergency. Everything inside me spilled out in those dire moments.

We never know how we will react in a situation until forced to respond under pressure. Sometimes that pressure comes from facing frightening or desperate circumstances. As the heat increases and the test ensues, we will find out how we think and move. Until then, we may never honestly know whether our faith or our fear will win in those moments.

> **"A faith that hasn't been tested can't be trusted."**
> **—Adrian Rogers**

REVEALING MORE OF WHO WE ARE

God wants us to understand who we are and what we have *in Him*. When we do, we can start grasping all we can have, do, and become in life. He has a way of revealing things for us to see for *ourselves*. How? By simply testing us. The testing process may be for a divine purpose. Still, it also allows us to see and discover things *for* and *about* ourselves. Sometimes the test can uncover what we are lacking. Other times it can make us more aware of what we already have and are capable of doing. Time and time again, life proves that our greatest strengths can often develop from tests involving pressure, pain, vulnerability, or weakness.

God used an ordinary night for me to encounter the strength, courage, and boldness I carried inside. When everything surfaced in those crisis moments, He wanted me to see and recognize what could stir up within me. He wanted me to know how strong I was. I had never been tested to that degree before. Strangely, I was engaged in what was happening *outside* me yet cognizant of what was happening *inside* me.

As I reflected more on the puzzling experience, I suddenly became aware of all that had transformed *inside* me through the years. Like a lightbulb illuminating, I realized the sharp contrast between the fearful and struggling woman I once was and the strong woman I had grown to be. Surprisingly, it was the incredible discoveries I'd made in the dark times that now equipped me to face life bravely. At the top of the list, I'd learned to use the strength of God inside me to powerfully influence my *own* life. As a result, I developed an inner force like never before.

As I paused in deep gratitude for my progress over the years, my mind unexpectedly flashed back to memories of painful events. Just the image of my once self-defeating existence caused my emotions to flicker. Yet deep down I knew those devastating times galvanized the power and strength I was walking in today. For some reason, my mind continued to press harder, determined to journey back in time to remind *myself* how far I had come.

Without warning, my thinking drifted back to the lowest point in my life. My body tensed up as I recalled how every day had been a fight to hang on to hope and to find the strength to keep going. I had never felt so lost, alone, stuck, and deeply depressed. I had become unrecognizable to myself. It was unquestionably the darkest period in my life.

The confident, independent woman I once knew had slowly melted away. The image of the adventurous, goal-setting girl barely out of her teens who had the guts to pursue her dreams had grown distorted. Daring to trailblaze her path in life, she took some bold risks. Living a courageous lifestyle, she traveled solo and performed her music internationally in elegant piano lounges. But sadly, I had become a shadow of who I once was. I had slipped into a muted middle-aged woman in a verbally and emotionally abusive marriage. Without a doubt, the pain had taken a toll on me.

I remember feeling like I was failing at everything in life. At the same time, the pain of an unknown future ahead seemed crushing. I tried hard to hold it together on the outside, but I was an utter mess on the inside. I felt myself slowly and secretly falling further and deeper into a pit. Everything I had worked so hard to achieve in my life seemed to disappear. I felt such a sense of loss. High anxiety and panic episodes began to set in, affecting my health and job. Every day was a struggle. As my voice was overrun and discarded, my inner world grew weaker daily. Everything in me was consumed with battling all the outside chaos.

I will never forget the shame and embarrassment that filled me at the thought of my second marriage falling apart. The confusion and humiliation had me so clouded and overwhelmed. God felt so far away. Everything I knew and believed about myself seemed to be fading. I was drinking more, trying to escape the reality of my life. I continually beat myself up in my thinking, ridiculing my judgment. I blamed myself for poor decisions and for falling into a situation that was so destructive. Even worse, I hated myself for being too weak to find a solution or pull myself out. Fear, anxiety, and panic attacks were escalating and had me trapped. What on earth had happened to me? I remember pleading with the Lord to help me find my way back to *me*.

STRONG AND COURAGEOUS
I remained in that dangerously dysfunctional marriage for over ten years until I finally dared to take control of my decisions and regain my life. As the divorce progressed, I focused intently on seeking God to help me rebuild my broken life. I asked Him to heal me and make me stronger than I had *ever* been. I never wanted to be so broken or fall so hard again. I knew God counsels us in Joshua 1:9, "This is my command—be strong and courageous! Do not be afraid or discouraged. For

the LORD your God is with you wherever you go" (NLT). But how do we get to that place of strength? I asked Jesus to show me how I could be strong and *stay* strong *inside.*

In faith, I took hold of my newfound freedom and began my steps forward. In less than a year, not only had my life healed and strengthened, but it had become more vibrant than it had been in a decade. For the first time, I grasped the true power of my choices and how they could shape my life daily. I was *talking to myself differently* and finally understanding how I could take control of my thoughts rather than them always controlling me. It was an important reset in my thinking. Most of all, I witnessed in awe how the power of God uniquely used *me* to influence and transform *me*. The more I leaned on Him, the stronger I became. As I stayed tuned in and faithful to actively doing *my* part, the power of the Lord working in me continued to blast through my weakness and kept me growing stronger.

As I focused on trusting in the Lord and learning to master my inner world, my outer world kept expanding. I became a top producer at my real estate office. I was active and socially involved at work and in the community. As my confidence grew, God soon opened another door and gave me the unwavering courage to take a leap of faith. I acquired and became the owner and CEO of an employment staffing and recruiting company. I worked hard and soon had hundreds of employees on the job. Within the first year, I reached a seven-figure revenue. I was now leading, speaking, training, and helping others face their struggles and challenges. My courage and strength soared as opportunity after opportunity opened up for me. God was helping me become the best version of myself, and I was finally living my best life.

CULTIVATING SIGNATURE SELF-TALK

At the lowest point in my life, the direction of my thinking had snowballed out of control. Where I was once a disciplined thinker, no amount of positive-thinking rituals or generic affirmations seemed to work anymore. It was as if they bounced off me and would not penetrate, especially when I needed them the most. Nothing could reach my negative self-talk deep inside or get to the root of my problems. I felt too weak and discouraged to pick up and read anything uplifting. When I failed or felt disappointed in myself, I was not kind. I had become my own worst critic. Behind closed doors, I felt empty when left alone. Yet through it all, I secretly longed to become my own greatest supporter, whether I was in the best of times or the worst.

The dramatic night the burglar alarm woke me was a gut-wrenching test. But instead of facing an intruder, something else showed up. I experienced a live demo of undeniable inner strength that surfaced from inside me. What fired up and poured out was unmistakable evidence that I had come a long way from drowning in weakness, overwhelm, and fear. I believe this is what God wanted me to see about *myself*. Remarkably, there could not have been a better test to let me witness with my own two eyes that the Lord had answered my prayer.

Life is a continual test of our faith. This book shares the game-changing practices that have helped me overcome deep trials. More importantly, it is a look at the profound ways God changed me in and through those dark seasons. In every journey, He rescued me from *me*. I asked Him to transform my life from the inside out, and God was faithful. He guided me to new places inside me that I never even knew existed. He helped and strengthened me to do things I never knew I could do. His love led me back to where I could love myself and others. What stirred up in me came alive like never before! More than just a lesson for a season, He gave me tools to equip me for a *lifetime*. The Lord led me to cultivate what I call my very own signature self-talk, which has allowed me to shape my thoughts, speak powerfully into my own life, and influence *myself* into action.

What do I mean by "signature self-talk"? I describe it this way: **specific one-of-a-kind self-talk I design and speak *out loud* to influence myself and improve my life. It represents the best of who I am and what I have to offer.**

To further explain, I create *personalized* self-talk messages for any change, boost, reset, or transformation I desire to make. I use my signature sound (which we will explore in chapter 7), style, and unique expression to convey my highly influential messages out loud. Putting it all into action, I stir up my gifts and fast-track results as I consistently move toward what I want to achieve. My signature self-talk is dynamic, distinguished, and a well-recognized part of my thinking. It has become an aspect of my core identity. As an athlete who would train her body, I actively train my *thinking* daily. Like building more muscle, every repetition in my signature self-talk regimen builds more *inner* strength. It helps me run steady and stay focused on my life priorities and goals.

> "Therefore I remind you to stir up the gift of God which is in you."
> —2 Timothy 1:6 NKJV

BUILDING A POWERFUL INTERNAL SUPPORT SYSTEM

It is often when we feel the least amount of power that we can gain the most insight into how God is building us stronger. But to get there, God will ask us to do our part, starting with our *thinking*. We are responsible for taking possession of what God has provided and promised us. What He supplies, He expects us to take action in *using*. Whether it's His strength and power inside us or our valuable gifts, talents, and creativity, we need to know how to stir these up daily. We will always have our part to do to activate our gifts and stay fortified inside. We determine if we will either rev up or shut down the flow of God in our life. One of the greatest lessons we can learn is that *His* part plus *our* part creates the powerful internal support system we need to create and live our best lives.

It was a defining moment when I stopped running *away* from my giants and started running directly *toward* them. My life was forever changed when I finally learned to take possession of and use what God had given me. What I discovered in my journey strengthened my faith and forged internal resources to help me stay prepared to do my part. As I developed a simple process to create and speak my signature self-talk, it became pivotal to helping me ignite my faith and influence my own thinking. I soon devised what I refer to as my self-talk arsenal, my stockpile of powerful, faith-driven messages to keep my internal support system strong. It was a matter of taking full responsibility for staying alert and being well-equipped *inside.*

God has given every one of us this same ability and authority to speak powerfully and to influence ourselves forward. The question is, how well do we use it? When we dare to use it to its full potential, our signature self-talk can elevate every area of our lives in exciting ways. We get to decide if we will build a hardy arsenal inside us and be well-prepared to do mighty things in life. Or will we choose idleness and risk not being ready when we may need stamina the most? Never before has the principle become so real that faith requires and will always require *action.*

BEHIND CLOSED DOORS
Our self-talk speaks to the very heart of who we are, as well as who we are becoming, *behind closed doors,* where we can struggle the most. Increasingly, as a society, we socialize online from home, work independently or remotely alone, lead alone, and build businesses alone. For many, there may also be seasons of living alone. As our culture moves us toward spending more time on our own, we can use this time as an opportunity to excel personally and professionally. We can make use of time alone to encourage ourselves in intentional ways.

God wants us to know how to make full use of the gifts He put inside us. We need to know that in His power we can take action, face pressure, stay in faith, think independently, and cheer on ourselves. We need to know *how* to pump ourselves up and calm ourselves down.

Learning how to use our signature self-talk as an activating force can help us prioritize what truly matters in our day, our performance, and our life.

In the pages ahead, I am sharing my playbook. I want to give away these faith-fueled God-inspired strategies that have worked so intensely in my life for over a decade, including my simple 4-Step DARE System. It will equip you to become zealous in spirit, well prepared for the pressures in life ahead, and primed to achieve more than you ever thought possible. Best of all, you can immediately start putting all these principles and practices to work. As you learn what it means to develop your own signature self-talk to speak compelling messages to yourself out loud, you will be ready to fire up and transform your life! You will discover, like never before, how to become a powerful influencer over your thoughts and actions. Most importantly, you will be well prepared to step into doing *your* part when God calls.

TRANSFORMATION AHEAD

I am excited for you to learn more about developing your *signature self-talk*. It can change your life, just like it did mine. As I began to create my powerful self-talk methods, I never imagined how deeply it would upgrade every area of my life, from my daily habits to my biggest goals and highest aspirations. It has become my number one means of controlling my thoughts, regulating my mind, and managing my mental health. Its primary purpose is to shape, direct, and activate *customized* messages to myself that can correct problem spots or change any area of my life for the better. The best part is that absolutely anyone can learn how to design their own self-talk unique to them, which we will be unpacking ahead.

It's important to clarify that in every chapter, the concepts introduced are based upon using our *God-given* power. Nothing could ever surpass the power of God working in us and through us. Nothing. Far beyond our limited strength, when we plug into God, we have an unlimited and almighty power source that exceeds anything we could ever do on our own. When our confidence is in Him, we can act and move confidently. He turns on the "enable" switch for every step we take to do *our part*. Even more, God supplies the perfect way for our thoughts to flourish in a sound, stable mind. What matters most is building our foundation upon the power of God as the underlying source.

With a solid promise that the Lord will show Himself strong for every one of us, the question remains: will we receive His power and actively use it? In good times or bad times, in drive or desperation, His flame stands ready for us to stir up. His Spirit stands ready to fill and empower us. His guidance is right beside us to show us the way. Will we allow these gifts to flow? Or will we ignore them and shut them down? It's time to wake up to what is alive and waiting for us. I am thrilled to show you how powerfully God can use *you* to influence *you*!

> **"And I pray that he would unveil within you the unlimited riches of his glory and favor until supernatural strength floods your innermost being with his divine might and explosive power."**
> **—Ephesians 3:16 TPT**

Are you ready to step into developing your signature self-talk? Are you pumped to see how God can use *you* to inspire, motivate, and transform *you*? Are you prepared to learn more about the authority and influence God has planted inside you? Are you excited to learn how to lead *yourself* and start fast-tracking more significant results in your life, career, and business? If so, let's get started on this life-changing journey of discovering, designing, and activating your signature self-talk!

Chapter 2

BUILDING A SOLID FOUNDATION

Have you ever played the game called Red Light, Green Light? It oddly resembles how we sometimes feel on the road to achieving *anything* in life. At the starting line, optimism fills the air. We are raring to jump into action. Bursting with anticipation, we can hardly wait for the game to begin. When the leader yells, "Green light," the race is on! You run as fast as you can toward the finish line. But watch out! When they call out, "Red light," you must immediately stop right where you are. Oh, and one important detail worth mentioning: if you fail to halt any movement, you can get sent all the way back to the starting line again! Whatever progress you made is wiped away and gone. Eventually, you may be able to celebrate a win at the finish line. But other times, all the starts and stops along the way wear you down enough to cause you to lose interest or stop trying altogether. Whether it's a fun, competitive game or actual life circumstances, many races we run are never won or even finished.

THE BATTLE OF INCONSISTENCY

Can you see how that stop-and-go process relates to what happens to us in so many of our efforts? Starting, then stopping, and having to start all over again. Getting back on track and running hard, only to fall off *again*! The road to our personal and professional development goals may sometimes feel like a bumpy game of Red Light, Green Light.

How often have you felt tripped up in a Red Light, Green Light game? Maybe life shifted when you got married, changed jobs, went through a divorce, or moved. Perhaps your whole world was turned upside down when you faced a health challenge or lost a loved one. Maybe you hit a point of resistance you couldn't get past, or got stuck in a rut circling the "forever familiar" lane. Life events can distract and derail you, whether it's something good or bad, an outside circumstance or an inside job.

Life can be tricky with so many twists and turns, and it can rack your journey with sudden starts and halting stops. It can be a struggle to continually jump in and out of your purpose. But the good news is that the more knowledge and tools you gain to equip you, the higher your chances are of making it back on track and *staying* on track. I am beyond excited to help you run a strong race, finish it, and even *win*!

STAYING THE COURSE

If you talk to people who've achieved any level of success, most will admit that it can be tough to stay on course sometimes. Whether sticking to a diet or starting a new business, you may wake up one day feeling ready to scale a mountain and conquer the world. But the next day, you pull the covers over your head and can't stand the thought of getting out of bed. One day you feel brave, vibrant, and invincible; another, you feel small and weak. You're not alone. It can be a constant battle to stay in the positive zone. Efforts can crumble when there is not a wall of courage, a fighting spirit, and deep inner strength.

Everyone can hit these potholes in the infamous road of life. We keep traveling the same streets and falling into the same traps repeatedly. But there is another choice. We can start following a *new* map and find a *better* way. It's time to recalibrate! This book will show you an alternate route to get you to the destination of your desired changes faster.

Have you hungered for a new plan to help you *stay* in a position of strength, even when you hit unexpected setbacks? Do you desire to be a more resilient version of yourself and to know how to hold *yourself* more accountable? When you decide to take charge of what's ahead in life's journey, you can be better equipped to guard against the downfalls. I'm talking about having powerful tools prepared, in hand, and ready to use. Your weakest days are certainly *not* the time to hunt for something that might help. Those days are the time to pull up the arsenal you've already built and apply it so you can stand firm.

THE EXCITING POTENTIAL FOR CHANGE

Not everyone realizes their powerful potential to upgrade their lives. Have you ever wished you could make more money, be more fit and healthy, feel happier, and thrive in every area of your life? Have you ever wanted to improve some habits or behaviors that drive you crazy?

Have you tried to overcome certain fears or depression, find more balance, or feel more in control of your life? For most, the answer would be an overwhelming yes! But knowing where to start or how to make genuine and *lasting* changes can be challenging.

Sometimes you need more time or energy even to look into finding solutions. If you hit an inspired moment, you might still debate if it will even be worth it. If you do manage to kick start an ambitious plan for your career, business, or personal life, there can still be trouble on the way to achieving your goals. Your mind might question how you will make your hard-earned changes stick in the long term. After all, how many repeated attempts have you made at self-improvement that eventually led right back to square one?

The fact that you have this book in your hands right now shows that you have a level of faith and grit different from most. It proves that you *continue* to take action. You belong to a special breed of *thinkers* and the driven few who genuinely get fired up to become more and achieve more in life. Even as you read these words, you are spending precious time and energy investing in your personal and professional development. You possess the success-minded spirit this book speaks to and connects with wholeheartedly. This season holds the promise of a breakthrough, and you are determined to show up for it!

MOUNTAINS TO MOVE

Growing and refining my self-talk evolved from wanting to solve my problem areas. However, it has now expanded into transforming *every* area of my life. I have used it in countless creative ways to shape my personal and professional ventures, from running my business to writing this book. My "signature self-talk" has become my greatest asset and most potent ally, from every cheer of victory to every needed restart in moments of devastating defeat.

It all started with identifying the thoughts that had been slowing me down. But ironically, I soon discovered that others also wrestled with these same thinking patterns. Sometimes it was a matter of a wrong mindset blocking the way. But more often it was not being able to get the *right* mindset into play. Either way, it all came down to one common denominator that kept many of us from achieving what we wanted. Plain and simple, it was *us* standing in the way. We had become so good at self-sabotage that we barely needed anyone else's help to whittle down our self-esteem. We did it quite well on our own. There were mountains *we* needed to speak to and move!

It becomes hard to place blame when we are operating as our own worst enemy. Our fearful, limiting, ever-critiquing inner selves can drag down our momentum at lightning speed. We develop sneaky little means of getting in our own way. Whether it's losing weight, paying off debt, or trying to succeed in business, we can develop habits and patterns that continually damage our results. Somehow, we become experts at stepping all over our own progress. Has that happened to you? Most of the time, we're the last to know or realize what we're doing to obstruct and ruin our outcome.

Unfortunately, this behavior usually doesn't stay contained to just one area or a one-time occurrence. It turns into a well-sculpted *thinking pit* that is all too easy to slip into repeatedly. The more we do it, the faster and easier we fall. Honestly, there is no more significant loss than a life sabotaged by one's *own* hands. It is a considerable loss when we shut down our dreams, lay down our purpose, and walk away from what is uniquely ours to do.

Since awareness is the key to turning things around and kick-starting positive change, let's take a daring look at a few areas of self-defeating behavior that can *keep* us on shaky ground. Not only can they catch us off guard, but they can also set us on the path toward the inevitable pit. I've experienced them all, and maybe you have too.

OBSTACLE 1: YOU GET ENTANGLED IN LIFE'S NOISE AND DISTRACTIONS

Our routine thinking jumps into action the minute we become conscious every morning and our feet hit the floor. We face whatever the day brings, things that are both in and out of our control. We take in all the voices we encounter along our day's path, including all the feelings attached. We move, go, feel, and live according to our old *default* settings. We rarely notice how much our time, energy, and focus are hijacked throughout the day. Can you relate to that?

As more days fall into this continuous cycle, our thinking patterns form and habits become set in stone. We silently allow it and freely participate in it, intentionally or unintentionally, consciously or unconsciously. We lose sight of how much our life controls us rather than us controlling our life. Eventually, where does all of this lead? It leads to our dreams and goals getting pushed aside, delayed, or run over. We don't choose; we comply.

Pressure builds, our health suffers, and negativity takes over.

You may not even realize this is happening to you until it is too late. One day you feel comfortably in control of your life; suddenly, all the voices around you become louder and more important than your own. You are drowning in the noise and pull of outer influences and obligations. It results in a lost connection with your hopes, dreams, goals, and desires. Giving into life's demands, you start to put *yourself* on the back burner. What you hope to accomplish in life gets buried deeper and deeper every day.

The pressure of people, places, and things becomes the *untamed* driving force of your life. Distractions pick up speed, pushing you further from pursuing a deeper purpose in your life. You enter the zone where you are no longer *making* life happen; life is happening *to* you. It feels like an endless spinning wheel. Daily, you keep surrendering your time, energy, and momentum. As the clock ticks on, it almost mocks all the missed opportunities that pass you by.

OBSTACLE 2: YOU CAN'T SEEM TO INFLUENCE *YOURSELF*

We all learn differently and take in information in our own unique way. You may be reaching for a wide range of expert voices to help you in your upward journey, but the question is, how close have you paid attention to your own influence? According to the *Oxford English Dictionary*, the definition of *influence* is "the capacity to affect the character, development, or behavior of someone or something." Even if you follow top-of-the-line people who spark your interest and feed you great ideas, can you influence *yourself* to move into action and apply those ideas? If not, doesn't it make more sense to spend your efforts looking *inward* to get your personal influence fired up *first*?

Getting lost in prioritizing everyone else's voice above your own can happen quickly or gradually. Either way, it's concerning when you look right past the one incredible person with the only *authentic* influence that holds *all* the power to take you to the next level. That would be *you*. It's always been you and will always be you who can effect real change in your life.

Maybe you don't feel skilled in influencing your own thinking. Or maybe you've been waiting for that day when someone's perfect words will fall upon your ears like a lightning bolt of great wisdom. Magically, it could finally do the trick to solve everything and get you moving. You may have been so busy looking around for answers that you looked right past your God-given *inner* wisdom and influence. What if God is waiting for you to *use* what He's already given you? What if what you're searching for already exists inside you? Imagine for one moment that you *already* possess everything you need to influence yourself into action to overcome whatever may be in front of you, whether it's fear, overthinking, perfectionism, imposter syndrome, or any other obstacle.

Once you genuinely access and conquer your inner world, all the things you've been unable to get yourself to do will finally break through—picture that! It is this exciting prospect that we will be looking at further in the chapters ahead. Although you may not be using it now,

God wants to unveil the mind-blowing power you hold to influence *yourself*.

OBSTACLE 3: YOU LOSE SIGHT OF IMPORTANT GOALS

This obstacle is big! We can become most frustrated when we're not accomplishing our goals. Most often, the primary reason for failing to achieve our goals in life is because they slip out of sight and out of mind. Isn't it astounding how we can let go of our future success over such a simple thing? Since we know that what we focus on grows, expands, and becomes more robust, it makes perfect sense that when we *stop* thinking about something, it soon shrinks and fades away, along with our drive and dedication to achieve it.

How can important things slip away from us so quickly? Think about all the times you saw or heard something so vital that you wanted to write it down urgently. It could be an eye-opening sentiment, a brilliant quote, or some encouraging words that hit the spot. It just touched you with a wow factor that moved something inside you. It could have grabbed your attention so profoundly that you fully intended to hold on to it, remember it, and let it *keep* inspiring you. But what did you do with it even after you were so excited to write it down and save it? Did it get lost under a pile, buried in a drawer, or maybe filed away in a messy notebook? Even if it earned a special place on the refrigerator or adorned your bathroom mirror, what gradually happened to its importance over time?

If we're honest with ourselves, many of our best collections of thought, including our own goals, as life changing as they seem, soon disappear from our sight and mind. We can even walk past them every day and no longer notice they are there. They eventually grow dim as they are overpowered, disregarded, and forgotten in the unending shuffle of life. So, what exactly causes valuable information to disappear from our thoughts? As simple as this: we stop looking at it and thinking about it.

BREAKING FREE
I understand it's painful to see ourselves caught in these scenarios. But at the same time, identifying the snare becomes the stake in the ground to start making an escape plan. There is no judgment here as I have undoubtedly fallen into every one of these traps myself, at one time or another. But my skills are now sharper because of it. I finally woke up to the fact that if I wanted a better life and different results, I had to start changing how I *talked* to myself, *influenced* my mind, and *retained* information. I also had to find a way to keep essential goals on my radar *daily* to stay focused on achieving them.

It was a revelation to learn that as I became the architect of my self-talk, it changed how I handled every one of the obstacles and self-defeating patterns I just described. I not only had to take control of my self-talk, but I also had to make an effective *plan* to start leading the way in my thinking. It became clear that my self-talk was brick by brick, constructing how I operated throughout my day. My self-talk was the *forerunner* that affected my attitude and actions. I had to decide if my dialogue, internal or external, would be positive or negative.

> "But each one must carefully scrutinize his own work [examining his actions, attitudes, and behavior], and then he can have the personal satisfaction and inner joy of doing something commendable without comparing himself to another."
> —Galatians 6:4 AMP

It takes courage to start examining your thinking, but it can be the key to some significant breakthroughs when you *dare* to be aware. When you start thinking about what you're thinking, it can pull dark hidden thoughts out and into the light. Only then can you begin to sort them out and take charge. When you do, you are on a path to knowing, liking, trusting, and influencing *yourself* like never before.

Understanding your thinking habits will help you recognize where to begin redesigning your self-talk. You will discover your top areas to target and prioritize. The more specific you are, the better. There is something more prominent in each of us than we are living right now. We must become students of *ourselves* if we want to find it and start living it!

BUILDING A STRONG HOUSE
Once I turned the corner in my thinking, it was time for reconstruction. The most crucial starting point in building anything is ensuring a solid foundation *before* the building begins. It's the key to making it *last*. So, before we step into the architect's role to design our signature self-talk, let's start at the bottom and build up.

If it's going to stand, every structure must have solid footing, or it will eventually fall apart. When we think of a house, the picture of a physical building on a permanent foundation usually comes to mind. But we must remember that a person can also be considered a "house." A person is a temple of God since the body is where a believer practices his or her faith. How often do we stop to reflect on the condition of our core foundation? Do we grasp the reality that each of us will exist in the house *we* design, build, and maintain? Even more importantly, what measures do we take to ensure our house *remains* solid and unshakable?

When we picture ourselves as a house, it brings a whole new dimension to that eye-opening proverb that tells us, "A wise woman builds her house, while a foolish woman tears hers down by her *own* efforts" (Proverbs 14:1 TLB, italics mine). How often do we think about how our efforts may be tearing down the house we live and breathe in daily? Have we stopped considering how our *self-talk* may weaken or damage our faith and the essence of who we are over time? Like unseen termites that slowly and quietly eat away at vulnerable structures, our destructive efforts can quietly take us down little by little. It may be time for a thorough building inspection, starting with examining and upgrading our *foundation*. Most importantly, let's get focused on how we not only build a sturdy house but must also maintain it.

THE THREE-PILLAR FOUNDATION
I have discovered that, without a doubt, the most robust "houses" are built on three foundational pillars. The strength of these three critical supports will determine how solid your house is and how well it will stand over time. The three pillars consist of how you talk to *God, yourself,* and *others.*

God wants our "house" and every part of our lives to be strong so we can get out there and be world changers. But as we know, we have *our part* to do in the building and maintenance of our house. We must consistently put our faith into action to keep influencing and fueling *ourselves*. We must keep stirring up and using all God has provided for us to stay in top condition. As we keep operating well in life, our sturdy "house" will speak volumes and become a beacon of light that God can use to help and inspire more and more people.

Let's take a closer look at the three foundational pillars and how each one plays a vital role in how your house will either thrive or barely survive.

PILLAR 1: HOW YOU TALK TO GOD
"Love the Lord your God with all your heart and with all your soul and with all your mind and with all your strength" (Mark 12:30 NIV).

First and foremost is how we talk to God. The entire basis of this book is reliant upon plugging into and *using* the strength and power of almighty God. Without a doubt, He must be *the* cornerstone for a sure foundation and the *first* pillar in place. Everything comes from His supernatural power and strength working *in* us and *for* us to help us create the best version of ourselves and an incredible life. Sometimes we wait to see ourselves differently before we come to God. But if we come to God first, *He* changes how we see ourselves.

The Lord is the *only* one who truly "gets" you and every part of your life story from beginning to end. He knows every breath you've taken, every laugh, and every tear. Every moment of your history and every single step and breath you will take ahead is known by Him alone. He is the only one who knows the *real* you and everything you've endured. God is the only one who knows *what* you need and *when* you need it. That's precisely why the Spirit of God is the starting point to help you *create* and *refine* the specific self-talk you need. Spirit-led self-talk is different from what you can generate on your own. He alone knows the life-giving words and messages you need to hear to influence your faith and move you toward all you are meant to do and become. He has already given you the tools to activate your powerful signature self-talk. Trust Him to guide you to put it all together as His voice intermingles with your voice. With God's help, you will shape your life more and more by how He leads you to talk to and influence *yourself*.

When we spend the time and effort to be alone with God, quiet and still, remarkable things begin to happen. We will see ourselves differently when we connect heart to heart in conversation with Him. When we see ourselves differently, we will talk to ourselves differently. The life you live on a day-to-day basis depends on what is happening *inside* you. Trust God to help you influence *yourself* in the right ways so you can accomplish more than you could ever dare to ask or even imagine. When you understand your need for God, it changes absolutely everything.

PILLAR 2: HOW YOU TALK TO YOURSELF
"For the whole law can be summed up in this one command: 'Love your neighbor as yourself'" (Galatians 5:14 NLT).

The strength of Pillar 2 depends upon how you talk to yourself, mainly since it directly influences how you will *love* yourself. If you don't love yourself, how can you truly love others? If you continually run empty inside, how can you cultivate great things to give or share with the world? God wants us to know how to rock our inner world and become strong and capable of *influencing* and *encouraging* ourselves. Why? Because it leads to loving ourselves. Our signature self-talk is the spark, fuel, and driver to build up our love and acceptance of ourselves. Spirit-led self-talk helps us develop the vibrant faith and belief system we need to think and live life abundantly.

How you talk to yourself becomes like marching to the beat of your own drum. You are moved more by what's *in* you than by what's around you. You no longer need to follow the crowd or conform to the world. Your voice's unique sound, tone, and expression become your signature instrument. The self-talk messages you create to speak out loud carry the sound of authority and influence that shapes your daily life. As you grow stronger and better equipped, your signature self-talk prepares you to help more people and make a difference in the world. When you know your value, you'll see everyone else's, too, which leads us to Pillar 3.

PILLAR 3: HOW YOU TALK TO OTHERS
"This is My commandment, that you love and unselfishly seek the best for one another, just as I have loved you" (John 15:12 AMP).

When Pillar 1 is solidly in place, you are rooted in truly knowing the Lord and connecting with Him. With

Pillar 2 secure, you stand firm and confident in knowing who you are and how to influence yourself. Finally, Pillar 3 holds an important position as you become established in talking to and relating to *others*.

Undoubtedly, you were born for a one-of-a-kind mission and purpose in this world. It is exciting to realize that as God works *in* you, He will shine more brightly *through* you. As your self-talk continues to refine, strengthen, and uplift who you are, your positive outlook will touch your relationships and improve how you talk to others. Your inner work prepares you to step into your unique way of impacting all the lives around you. Everything you become on the *inside* will directly affect your relationships.

How we speak and communicate with others determines how we are perceived and the impact we make. Regardless of our physical appearance or ability to make a fabulous first impression, who we are *inside* becomes revealed every time we open our mouths. It's only a matter of time before our inner condition eventually surfaces. But when we authentically honor God and love ourselves, we are well-grounded in our internal support system. Although never perfect, how we live, treat, and serve others turns into a heart mission and an investment we *care* about making. Beyond any material things in this world that will soon disappear, our love for others is real and eternal.

As we love GOD, we see ourselves differently.
As we love OURSELVES, we see others differently.
As we love OTHERS, we view life differently.

BUILDING A SOLID FOUNDATION

Ultimately, how we relate to God, ourselves, and the world around us means everything to keeping our house solid and stable. Strength and power will flow when we take responsibility for choosing wisely and building on the *proper* foundation.

Now, I have a question for you. How is *your* foundation? If it is cracked, leaking, or slowly deteriorating, it could be time to get your house in order with some upgrades. It may be time to stabilize your footing and strengthen your structure. Or it may be time for a complete remodel. Either way, it begins with your decision to build your house on a *solid* foundation. When you do, watch how your life soars in all the right ways!

Next, what could a loaded dare have to do with your self-talk? Let's find out as we zoom in closer to examine *why* our self-talk is so critical.

Chapter 3

WHY SELF-TALK MATTERS

Should I jump? A hidden camera secretly spied on people in the agony of that decision at the top of a ten-meter-high platform. Men and women, young and old, were drawn like a magnet into the challenge of conquering the nerve-rattling jump. One by one, they climbed up three steep metal ladders at an indoor pool to face their *own* dare. As they reached the top for the first time, the shock on many of their faces was evident as they slowly peered down. They just stood there, silently processing the dramatic drop. As reality sunk in, an *inner battle* had clearly begun. The struggle was apparent as they weighed their options. Would they take their private dare and follow through? Or would they turn around and quietly climb back down?[1]

It seemed that the self-talk for many of them involved a high state of alert. Something appeared to shift inside them after boldly climbing the ladder and reaching the top. The *new* perspective, looking down at the water below, intensified the risk. They looked stuck and plagued with indecision. Would they be able to go through with it? A few carefully tiptoed to the edge and then stiffly backed up. The minutes ticked by as their faith and their fear collided.

An internal debate seemed to continue as each swimmer attempted to talk themselves *into* or *out of* making the frightening jump. Mixed emotions began to erupt as some laughed awkwardly or even cursed. Before long, many returned to silently staring at the water as they tried to get their courage in gear. The camera caught it all as the inner battle raged on and the story unfolded, moment by moment, during this captivating study on how human beings face fear.

Only a couple of brave souls finally tapped into their courage to make the big jump. Not surprisingly, several gave up and abruptly climbed back down the steep ladders. Disappointment, frustration, embarrassment, and even anger seemed to emerge as they accepted their glaring defeat.

This intriguing *New York Times* video, "Ten Meter Tower," was revealing. What interested me the most was witnessing the kind of self-talk that surfaced *out loud* as they stood at the top facing their *own* dare—even more, how this audible self-talk dramatically affected the final results. The camera caught the following types of statements from those who eventually failed to make the jump: "This is impossible!" "Forget it!" "It's a long way down!" "No, I don't have the guts for this."

Interestingly, the sentiments of the few who made the jump were opposites. Here are some of the words spoken out loud and caught by the camera: "Let's do this!" "Go, girl!" "Be positive; it's fun!" "Right, here we go!" Far beyond a simple difference in words, it was a different kind of self-talk and a different state of mind. It was evident that their self-talk played a decisive role. It *influenced* their decision either to step forward and jump or to step back and abort their mission. In the end, they talked *themselves* into jumping. It was fascinating to see how their spoken words inevitably matched the outcome every time.

> **What can you truly accomplish in life if you can't influence yourself?**

WHEN FAITH AND FEAR COLLIDE

At one time or another, most of us have encountered someone who dared us to do something risky. If we were honest, most of us would also admit that a *dare* has a remarkable way of causing us to act on impulse, whether it's to show our courage, prove a point, or even settle a score. But what happens when we dare *ourselves* to do something risky? Does that same trigger go off? How often are we willing to plunge in and prove to *ourselves* that we can do something?

Your challenge may not be facing the dare of a ten-meter jump, but imagine if God suddenly opened a massive door of opportunity in your life that required a great deal of courage. How would you handle the fears you would need to confront? Would you dare *yourself* to take that leap of faith? Or would you avoid it, walk away, or even run in the opposite direction? Still more wondrous, would you have even dared to *ask* God for that big door of opportunity in the first place? Do you usually talk yourself into or out of moving forward in anything that feels unfamiliar, risky, or scary? The big question is, how does *your* self-talk show up to influence you when your faith and your fear collide?

**Either your faith will overcome your fears,
or your fear will overcome you.**

It becomes clear that our outcome can be profoundly influenced by what we tell ourselves and believe about ourselves and our situation. Just as shocking is realizing how much our self-talk can affect us as we are in the middle of doing something. For instance, if we are in motion and then begin to think about or talk about our anxiety, fear, or weakness, it can manifest in real time and stop us from doing what we set out to do. Even worse, our negative self-talk can start to multiply and grow. Has that happened to you before? Has your harmful self-talk ramped up and *increased* your fear and negativity *while* you were in the act of something important?

Once we understand and grasp the impact our self-talk can have on us at any moment, we will be more determined to use it wisely. We can master and stabilize our self-talk to work to our benefit rather than leave it entirely to chance. When we want successful outcomes, it pays to plan excellent self-talk to match our desired results. Like each jumper whose own dialogue contributed to their mindset at the top of that ten-meter platform, we have an endless choice of the talk *we* generate. We can either speak words of encouragement to ourselves or speak to the negative. We can talk ourselves into or out of whatever it is we hope to do. Which way does *your* self-talk typically lean?

WORDS ARE INFLUENTIAL
I dare you to become keenly aware of observing this powerful connection between your dialogue (both internal and spoken) and your results. Consider a closer look at the times you started out with your thoughts dialed into how anxious and stressed you felt, how difficult things looked, or how you were not up to the task. How did it turn out? We know our *words* can have a lasting effect on others, but we forget that they can also have a powerful and lasting effect on *us*!

To drive home the point, here is a quick experiment you can do with simple words, comparing the negative versus positive impression. I want you to see how even one individual utterance can affect you. Words can also play a part in your mood and your state of mind. Even one word can influence how you think or feel. Let's put a few words to the test. Focus on and *slowly* say these four words *out loud,* one at a time: tired, hopeless, defeated, failure. Repeat them again slowly. How do these words land in your mind and your spirit? How do they make you *feel*?

Now, focus on and *slowly* say these four words *out loud,* one at a time: strength, power, believe, champion. Repeat them again slowly. Do you feel any difference? Even simple little words can have a high impact. More than just the spoken word, your mind pulls up specific images and attaches emotions to them. The bottom line is that the words we use can profoundly influence us. Proverbs 18:21 tells us, "The tongue has the power of life and death" (NIV). Therefore, we want to be more conscious of what we say and *purposely* pick words that will work in our favor. Keep this vital connection in mind as you learn more about using your self-talk to work *for* you rather than against you.

SELF-TALK IS CRITICAL
You may not realize it, but you talk to yourself all day. We all do. We have an internal database of memories, experiences, pains, and pleasures on tap that make up and influence our daily thinking. Your self-talk is *constant*, and it can range from silent inner thoughts to dialogue out loud. Sometimes that little voice in your head can be soft and quiet. Other times it can be loud and passionate. Your self-talk is unique, highly personal, and a particular language you know and recognize. It often becomes so automatic that you may rarely be aware of it. Although it's completely private, and you may ignore it, what your self-talk produces *in* you can surface *outside* you as well. In other words, it can impact your mood, behavior, and interactions. It has a funny way of rippling through every part of both your inner and outer worlds.

When you are brave enough to zoom in and take a closer look, you will realize there are indeed existing patterns in how you talk to yourself. You may even be stunned as you connect the dots and begin to see how much your routine self-talk has undermined your confidence, damaged you, or held you back. As you zoom out to the bigger picture, you may realize how much your self-talk has been digging into your ability to be the person you want and hope to be.

Before I developed my signature self-talk, I kept getting stuck in the same places. I had to deal with some patterns of thinking that had sneaky little ways of tripping me up. I traveled a circle of the same thoughts that would pop up and cause me to stumble again and again. They stripped me of power and blocked me from using my mind to motivate and drive myself further. Although I was always a hard worker, my thoughts had a way of slowing me down. Like a wandering ship, how I spoke to myself often lacked clear direction or intention. The standard procedure for my day was to do my best to process whatever life threw my way. Some days were a doozy! The ups and downs were wild and kept me on an emotional roller coaster. I was unaware of how lost I was in my thought life. Have you ever felt that way?

When my eyes were finally opened, I gained some helpful new tools, but something *still* needed to be added. Whether I tried to read positive and encouraging statements or repeat a list of affirmations, my attempts felt generic, distant, lukewarm, and impersonal. They didn't directly address my unique situation, problems, hopes, or dreams. It was a struggle to tune in and focus on them with repetition. Before long, they were buried and overrun by my crazy busy life. I didn't have the time or motivation to keep repeating a series of "I am" statements from a piece of paper every day or look over a list of goals. Basically, reading words on a page did not bring them to life in my heart or mind. I needed a faster and simpler process that I could stick with. I also wanted it to be more personal, meaningful, and vibrant.

Time after time, what I was trying to plant and grow in my mind failed to take root or produce anything of substance. I was caught in a circle of defeat until I *finally* discovered how to craft my signature self-talk. This was the start of learning that I could design my self-talk messages in specific ways to make them my own. I realized it's much more than putting *any* good seeds in my mind. It was about implanting my *own* signature seeds. Even more, I had to pay attention to *how* they were planted. This was the phenomenal turning point.

SIGNATURE SELF-TALK IS UNIQUE
Whether you realize it or not, you possess one-of-a-kind *signature* features in every part of you. After all, you are an original. You have signature strengths, creativity, and talents. Look at how your handwritten signature is even a self-styled expression of your name. Like every other part of you, it's uniquely your own. You get to design how it will appear and to control and authorize how, when, and where you will use it. Just ask your bank; your signature carries great power and authority and the ability to secure essential aspects of your life. It is handcrafted by you, the artist and creator, and it is precious. It's your personal stamp, legal trademark, and a physical impression and representation of *you*. It is yours to direct and use in countless ways throughout your life to accomplish great things.

The qualities of your signature self-talk are not only original and unique to you but also set apart and incomparable to your usual chatter. It is dialogue intentionally created *by* you and *for* you. Once you decide on the specific purpose you want to use it for, it is *your* masterpiece to build. Whether you focus on fitness plans, career goals, or financial gain, your signature self-talk can surpass any generic affirmation or positive thinking cliché. It can accomplish far more than any short-lived *outer* hype can do for you. What you generate from the *inside* of you will always be more effective and more sustainable.

The real magic lies in formulating your own *signature messages*. When you incorporate your specific details, trigger words, and personal passion for making it your own, the signature self-talk you design is unlike any other. Only you can take your self-talk out of auto mode and set it into gear. When you start molding it and directing it to a specific purpose, it transforms from a one-size-fits-all option into a one-of-a-kind solution. You upgrade and align it with your personal circumstances, needs, and desires. You clarify it, you sharpen it, and you control it. When you create your signature self-talk to be spoken out loud with extreme purpose and personal meaning, you can be assured that the effect will be deeply rooted.

Your signature self-talk encompasses everything familiar to you that your mind distinctly understands. It involves tapping into the unequaled power of resonating with *yourself*. You use your individual experiences, personality, insight, and flow as you draw out the best of you to influence and transform your own life. You learn to put God's strength and power to work in your life, using your own voice as He leads.

It can be far too easy to get into the habit of looking around to find answers in life instead of looking *inward*. God lives *in* you. That's where He can be found. That's where He influences you and shows you how you can influence *yourself*. When you understand the power of producing your own unique messages and master the techniques, it can revolutionize your self-talk and your life. Of everything God can use to change your life, I am convinced He can most powerfully use *you* to transform you!

SELF-TALK AFFECTS YOU
Our self-talk determines the quality of our life. It affects every one of our habits, our ambitions, and our ultimate destiny. So often, we don't pay attention to how much our unmonitored self-talk shapes us. However, when we form and use our *signature self-talk*, it can interrupt and replace wayward thoughts. We can design *new* pathways to upgrade our thinking, spark new energy, and create momentum. Essentially, we put the *powerhouse* of our minds to work like never before. It takes practice, but living our best life every day is well worth the investment.

Has negative self-talk been creeping in and causing you to feel overwhelmed or out of control? Although we are all bound to experience some deep valleys or unexpected storms, we can't afford to stay stuck in negativity. We can't allow our self-talk to bully us or overpower the progress we've made. We can be determined to get to the heart of our intentions, the root of any problems, and the blocks holding us back. When we do, we move full swing into cleaning our "house" and taking back lost territory!

You may have already developed healthy self-talk and a positive state of mind. If so, don't stop there! It's important to keep using your empowered self-talk in even more profound and significant ways. Like a toned muscle, it takes ongoing effort to keep it firm. Every season of life can bring unseen challenges that can test your self-talk in new ways. Therefore, the goal is to *stay* mentally tough with a fully prepared self-talk arsenal.

BUILDING A HEALTHY SELF-TALK DIET

The collection of people, places, things, and experiences in our lives seems to melt together and become the "stuff" that affects what eventually comes out of us. We usually don't sort through or clean out our "collection" very often, so it keeps piling up and showing up, even if we don't want it to. Our thinking will usually tip to the negative first because the most painful and hurtful events always seem to stay close to the top of the pile. We may have to dig down to find the positive pieces of our collection because they can get buried quickly and easily.

Like starting a new healthy diet, your signature self-talk will change what you feed yourself daily. If you've ever had old recordings go off or continually play in your mind, your louder and more determined signature messages can step in to be the powerful remix. You can masterfully design a new viewpoint and set the record straight. There are moments in life to let go of, and incredible moments to hold on to. I bet you already know which ones you should be freely playing over and over again. Your signature self-talk can help you turn *on* preferred settings to remember the people, places, and things in your life that have strengthened you. Likewise, you can turn *off* the painful moments that are past and gone. They serve no purpose other than to weaken and upset you.

Becoming aware of and controlling your thinking is one of the most significant investments you will ever make. Think about how much mental and emotional energy is wasted on what you can *never* control. Consider the massive benefits of a renewed focus on what you *can* control. There are so many valuable things worth remembering in life, yet that space can get eaten up by holding on to the wrong things. Even the oldest and most engrained recordings stuck on play inside you can be tackled and changed. It is a matter of designing a *new* narrative and firing up your *signature* message in order to start overpowering the old, destructive one. No self-talk playlist should pop up or play without your express approval.

CONDITIONING YOUR MIND

When you *choose* your focus and what you consume in your thought life each day, you begin *actively* conditioning your mind. In fact, you will grow more and more sensitive to and aware of negative, harmful, or unhelpful influences. All the more, you will get good at dealing with them. Something in you will instinctively rise up to question or reject them. You will develop new strengths and the ability to make better choices on a *thinking* level. You will get to the point where it will be natural to quickly catch, correct, and redirect wayward thoughts. What once used to slip right by you (or *into* you) no longer gains easy access. Your mind progressively forms *higher-quality* habits to work in your best interest.

As you realize there are choices of influence to weigh, you begin to pause and think *before* taking action. You have a new protocol for checking to find out what each option contains. Why? Because you are now paying closer attention and caring more about making *good* decisions. It has become essential for you to get a better result than before. You have a clearer vision of all the fantastic benefits you will receive when your empowered self-talk is part of your regular everyday routine.

As you take a decisive step to regulate your mind, a good measurement of your progress is how often you stop and ask yourself, "How will this really affect me?" You learn to put up a guardrail, a new boundary, and develop a rigorous new thought process. You become more assertive and wiser as you increase your speed and accuracy in choosing what to put in your good versus bad thinking buckets. You sharpen your skill in knowing what to accept and what to reject. You not only grasp a new understanding of what will build you up but also what can deplete you. Best of all, you gain a new authority over managing your thoughts. You are pioneering a path of conditioning your mind to grow more selective and forceful in how you direct your thinking.

CHANGING YOUR INNER FILTER

Study after study confirms that *what* we tell ourselves affects everything we do—our health, relationships, and success, to name a few. On an even deeper level, the way we process incoming information is shaped by what can be considered an *inner filter* deeply ingrained in us. It has been meticulously constructed from our lifetime of experiences. Whatever comes at us in life, that fragile little filter goes to work to give its own spin or meaning. It throws everything together in a split moment and comes up with our unique *perspective.* Like an assembly line, that perspective moves right down the conveyor belt into creating our feelings and forming an eventual response to whatever happened. But again, it's all based on what our own little inner filter *invented*. The big question is, how trustworthy is our internal filter? What kind of condition is it in? If it is responsible for shaping everything in a way that will either help or hurt us, we need to know! Is it really based on truth? Or has it become dirty and clouded over time?

Think for a moment about how your inner filter has been serving you. Has it gradually drifted off course and skewed your thoughts? Sometimes it can even try to reject *quality* people, places, or things that are good for you. Does it continually twist and turn life events to spark confusion and stress or make you feel upset? Does it tend to take small things and blow them up to seem much more monumental and overwhelming? It may even concoct negative signals from people or situations you encounter. It could be time to clean the lens you see through and correct the damage it has been causing.

Imagine if you could effectively recalibrate or even reinvent your inner filter. How valuable is it to you to have your filter in tip-top shape so that it will *accurately* process information with calm confidence and sound judgment? It is possible to reset your inner filter to serve as your faithful ally, not your enemy. A friend, not a foe. In fact, your signature self-talk can be the starting point to switching your filter off autopilot mode and onto a new setting that can make your life easier, not more difficult. You can begin to shape that inner filter by crafting what *you* want it to look and function like inside you. You can tear down your old filter piece by piece and replace it with a new God-given filter of the highest quality at any time.

REFRAMING YOUR THINKING

Your self-talk can come into powerful play as you stop to question and challenge your *own* thinking. You can run a tight ship and expose the lies and obstacles that will no longer be tolerated. You have the absolute power to tell your mind *precisely* what you will think and believe. Whether it's becoming more purpose-driven, generating more meaning in your life, or motivating yourself, everything starts with *you* taking charge. You can also draw a line in the sand and establish limits that will no longer allow manipulation to play in your thoughts.

Whatever life throws your way, be assured that you can design a productive response. If you are hurt, disappointed, or feel defeated, you can craft a positive counterthought that works *for* you rather than *against* you. Please don't allow your pain to grow into bitterness, which can rob your peace. Instead, you can frame any difficulty in a way that will make you more determined and resilient. It's not about ignoring or pretending the bad doesn't exist; it's about processing it *wisely*. More than simply choosing not to *stay* in a negative thought, make every effort to find at least one meaningful way to turn it around and make it work *for* you. Be determined to take extreme ownership of your own life lessons.

Our most prominent life tools can develop out of our most difficult times. It's all in how we *position* our thinking. We often forget that we have every right to choose exactly how we want to frame something. We get to choose. We don't have to accept surface appearances or even how we feel. We can dig deeper to find and focus on a hidden positive over any negative.

YOUR CELLS ARE LISTENING

Finally, let's examine one more critical reason to get our thinking, self-talk, and responses to a healthy, thriving place. Although we don't often focus on it, developing a solid *inner core* will directly affect our physical wellness. It has been proven that the cells in our body actually *respond* to what we say, what we hear, and how we feel. Although we may not even be aware, our cells are *always* tuned in to listen and react. They are constantly affected by what is happening *in* us and *around* us. We must realize how much positive and negative events in our inner world actually impact our *physical* body.

The mind-body connection is vital to our well-being. Whether based on the past, present, or future, thoughts and worries affect our biology and wellness at the deepest level. With this in mind, it becomes even more important to guard and protect our thought lives and keep our mental state strong. God calls us to be transformed by the renewing of our *minds* (Romans 12:2). We can now see that on an even grander scale, God's *internal* restoration can extend far beyond our minds and into *every* part of us, right down to our cells!

LEARNING TO FIX YOUR MIND

Now that we understand how we are deeply impacted by every thought, we can begin to understand the sheer wisdom in God telling us to *fix* our minds. He wants us focusing not just on random good things but on *specific* types of thoughts that He outlines as being of the *highest* benefit. They serve a deep purpose in building a thought muscle that keeps pulling from the richness of life and the goodness of God. It's like a secret recipe to create the ultimate inner environment of joy, contentment, gratefulness, and peace, to name a few. We're told to think about *"whatever* is true, . . . noble, . . . right, . . . pure, . . . lovely, . . . admirable—if *anything* is excellent or praiseworthy—think about such things" (Philippians 4:8 NIV, italics mine).

With this in mind, creating your *own* influential signature playlists makes perfect sense to help you focus your thoughts. This will help you fix your mind and keep it anchored on good things. For example, consider the times you were relentlessly courageous in overcoming a challenge. The way you made an invaluable difference in someone's life, or the feeling of achieving a hard-earned goal. These are excellent and praiseworthy memories and can help you build your faith, courage, and confidence for the battles you may face yet ahead.

Never let your epic moments and the good things God has done in your life grow dim or be forgotten. Every part of you adds a piece to the puzzle of who you are and what your life will become. You have rich stories and praiseworthy successes that deserve to be memorialized and told repeatedly *in your mind.* You can grow sharper and wiser when strategically *fixing y*our thoughts. Like setting a thermostat, you can learn to program your thinking with purpose in order to keep returning to a fixed position—a specific, predetermined place for keeping you in a state of comfort, health, and wellness.

Buckle up for the next chapter, which lays out the incredible power of influencing yourself. It's time to light the fire *inside* and take control of what you *will* and *will not* allow to affect you.

Chapter 4

INFLUENCING YOURSELF

With life hanging in the balance, a cardiac surgeon carefully removed a patient's heart to repair it. After returning it to the chest, he began the usual process of gently massaging the heart back to life. But it wouldn't start beating on its own. The medical team proceeded to administer more extreme measures but to no avail. No matter what they tried, the heart wouldn't start beating. Finally, the surgeon knelt beside the patient and quietly spoke directly into her ear: "This is your surgeon, and your heart has been repaired. Now *tell* your heart to beat again." Remarkably, at that very moment, her heart began to beat.[2]

I was riveted by the story of this actual event. It captured the very essence of how powerful our *own* influence can be. It is astounding how our body reacts to what we think and say to ourselves, spoken or unspoken. Our God-given ability to influence *ourselves* is a miraculous force, from activating our hearts and minds to moving every intricate part of us.

DEVELOPING YOUR SIGNATURE INFLUENCE

You, my friend, are your most significant *influencer*. You hold the inherent power and authority to influence *yourself*. You always have, and you always will. You only have to step into knowing how to use your extravagant influence in new and exciting ways. Like the beating heart in this incredible story, you must stir up and *awaken* what's inside you. God put *you* in charge of yourself! You have to start recognizing that the ultimate influence in your life is *you*. After all, you are the sole expert on yourself. Your thoughts, beliefs, words, and voice stand ready to communicate the defining messages for your life. You merely have to activate them. It's time to rise and shine!

The most important relationship we have on this earth is with *ourselves*. One of the most incredible ways to nourish that relationship is to get engaged in developing our self-influence. When we do, we take actual ownership of our strengths, flaws, and decisions that make us who we are every day. We step into better control over how we want to think, where we want to go, and what we plan to accomplish. It's up to *us* to determine how outside influences positively and negatively affect us. Most of all, we must watch that they are not quashing or damaging the authority we should have over *ourselves*.

What is your mind starting and stopping in you? What do you want to set in motion or bring back to life inside you? As the surgeon's experience beautifully spotlights, you can influence yourself spiritually, mentally, emotionally, and even physically. Think of all the new ways you can *tell* your heart, mind, and soul to start supercharging your life!

INFLUENCING YOUR BEHAVIOR
In 2021, it was shocking to hear that the life expectancy for Americans had experienced the most sizable drop since World War II. According to CDC's National Center for Health Statistics (NCHS), the expected longevity fell by eighteen months.[3] How could this be? What about all the research, studies, technology, and advancements in almost every field over the decades? While we have come so far in breakthrough developments, Americans' degree of hope and ability to withstand the pressures of life appear to be declining. Drug overdoses and suicide continue to rise. People are giving in and giving up on life in higher and higher numbers.

The first place we face life's battles is deep within ourselves. When life hits hard, what do we say to ourselves? What happens behind closed doors when we face the personal challenge of dealing with our thoughts? Even with the most caring support system around us, we alone are the ones who handle our inner world. We are the *only* ones who get to pick how we will speak to and treat ourselves.

Our self-talk deserves our attention. It can't be left to chance. Sometimes we forget that *we* get to form each day—what we see, what we think, and what we decide it means. Each moment we determine if we will accept or reject who we are. When we build and strengthen our *inner* core, we can be empowered to face whatever may happen *outside* us.

There will always be times we don't understand our behavior. We make mistakes. We do what we don't want to and don't do what we should be doing. We get distracted and put things off. We avoid or procrastinate. Isn't it good to know that we can always decide on a better direction and start making changes at *any* time? As we get clear on identifying what needs to change, our own powerful influence can kick in and start making it happen.

Influencing yourself is more than a form of self-discipline. It's more than a tidy dos-and-don'ts checklist to stay in control. The ability to influence yourself goes much deeper. It penetrates your feelings, desires, and passions at the most profound level. It puts the intense influence of your own thoughts, words, and voice into action in real time. Just as we spend time building any relationship, the more time we spend positively influencing *ourselves*, the more potent that influence will be. Our personal power will grow as we continue to work *in* and *on* ourselves.

OWNING YOUR INFLUENCE

When you continually look to people or something *outside* you to validate and encourage, motivate, and strengthen you, it's easy to grow dependent upon them. Instead of taking any measures to generate positive influence inside yourself, you rely upon others to prop you up from the *outside*. You can put so much stock in other people that you begin to discount your own influence. You can get into the habit of looking *outside* yourself to help you *feel* the way you want to feel. Although it may seem more accessible to find something nearby to lift your spirits or trigger your motivation, what the world gives can be taken away unexpectedly. The people and things around you can change anytime, and your supply chain can quickly dry up.

When you take hold of your *own* influence, you start telling *yourself* the words you've been giving others the job of telling you. You master your own messaging and how you speak to yourself. Instead of *outside* boosts to feed you daily, what God supplies *inside you* provides everything you need for a lifetime!

MASTERING SELF-INFLUENCE
Throughout history, there have been inspiring stories and examples of people who had the uncanny ability to profoundly influence *themselves*. It showed up in their staunch refusal to give in or give up. Their inner driving force was tested in extraordinary ways, especially in the face of personal rejection. Others in similar situations may have called it quits, but they somehow maintained a *different* kind of self-influence.

Famous examples include Abraham Lincoln, who lost election after election before becoming a US president, and Walt Disney, who was turned down repeatedly and told he "lacked imagination" before his success with Disney, along with many others, from celebrities to top-selling music artists to wealthy business moguls.[4] Many of them carry painful stories of how they were once cruelly rejected, yet somehow they were able to influence themselves to keep going. It was what they generated *within* that was the driving force. They pressed on and refused to quit until they finally found their break.

Hearing the long, harrowing journeys of successful people in the world can be surreal. The highly regarded person we see doesn't seem to match the inner struggles they describe in their story. It can be heart-wrenching to hear them confess how they kept going in the face of terrible ridicule and resounding failure. We wonder how they dared to keep taking risk after risk, sometimes on the verge of losing everything! They each had their own way of using what was meant to stop or crush them. They were able to turn it around to produce their own breed of empowerment. It was their self-influence and inner strategy at work that kept pushing them forward. It was a moment-by-moment, day-by-day transformation. Eventually, their resilience caused them to show up in a way that could not be denied. As they continued to influence themselves, it changed who they were and what they were able to accomplish.

Just like these diehards influenced themselves to find their way to success, we can also engage our self-influence in profound ways. When the battle hits hard in every direction, we can learn to draw masterfully from our own God-given inner resources. Not just to conquer the present rejection or defeat we face but to build even greater reserves. God can take all the broken pieces and skillfully weave them together for our good. It's a matter of being well armed to face adversity. In fact, we can decide to keep growing more dynamic because of it. Our self-influence can continue to become more skilled and resilient every day, no matter who or what comes against us.

INFLUENCING YOUR POTENTIAL

How often do we keep an invisible list of everyone we expect to support, encourage, and help us in life? We want the people around us to recognize and pay attention to how we feel. After all, if they really love us, they should always care about cheering us on to reach our highest potential, right? So be honest; what happens inside you when the family members or friends you counted on don't show up? Where are you left when those closest to you don't seem to understand how you feel, what you're doing, or what's important to you? How do you cope when you sense that you are standing entirely alone? We all have expectations of how we want others to talk and respond to us. In fact, we may even dream up what we would like them to say to generously praise our efforts or even push us a little harder.

But at some point, we must stop and ask ourselves, how does my own voice rate in its ability to make me feel inspired and deeply supported? What do I expect to hear from *myself*? How am I rooting for *myself*? How much weight does *my* voice hold compared to everyone else on the list I consider to be of high value? Most of all, have I been giving more power to every voice around me over my own?

While there are endless people and things in this world that can attempt to block you from reaching your potential, nothing can stand in your way more than you can stand in your own way. Someone or something may try to deter you, but only you hold power and control over your own growth. It is not up to other people or other things. It is 100 percent in you and up to you. Nothing the world can say or believe can influence you as deeply as what *you* say, do, and think about *yourself*. Your ability to impact your own thoughts can never be underestimated. Ultimately, your mind will believe what *you* are telling it.

When you set out to do anything significant in life, there will always be a voice trying to hold you back. Just make sure it's not your own!

UPGRADING YOUR INFLUENCE

Whenever you wish, you can upgrade your self-influence with your own self-talk messages. You have a sort of *internal design studio* available to you at all times. In this secret little place inside, you get to create the dominant signature self-talk that *you* pick to tell yourself. It's up to you to step up to the control panel and change the settings. Instead of telling yourself, "Who do you think you are even trying this?" you *decide* to say to yourself, "Hey, be confident; you've got this!" You have everything you need to craft *new* thoughts that will influence the life experiences you desire.

When you take full responsibility to influence, uplift, direct, and motivate *yourself*, you shift that expectation off everything *outside* you. It's a matter of realizing that no matter how many voices speak into your life every day, God has given *you* the voice that holds the *ultimate* influence. When you harness the power of that influence, you can build thoughts that can transform any area you want to change. "For as he thinketh *within himself*, so is he" (Proverbs 23:7 ASV, italics mine). You can master and speak boldly to your inner voice and knock down the blocks that have been so sneaky at shifting positives to negative. Your self-influence can overpower old destructive impulses and mindsets. Just like you choose what apps to use on your smartphone, you will decide what signature apps you will run every day on your "smart mind."

When you know how to influence yourself effectively, you can start moving the needle on fulfilling more of your potential. There is indescribable freedom in moving expectations *off* others and *into* your own responsibility. It takes you out of the passenger seat and into the driver seat of your influence. You get to shift into a higher gear and speed toward what encourages, motivates, and fires you up. You get savvy about steering clear of whatever brings you down, distracts you, and discourages you. You get to crank the volume of the good tunes you want to hear everywhere you travel. Most of all, you choose all the destinations and the route to get there!

TAKING AUTHORITY OVER YOUR AUTHENTIC VOICE

Once you tap into the power of your own signature influence, staying true to your *authentic* voice is more important than ever. Have you ever toned down speaking confidently or held back on sharing your opinions only to accommodate others? How often have you pushed aside expressing your feelings based on how others *might* react? Was there ever a time when you didn't speak up even though you had considerable expertise? God has given you the *authority* to live courageously and authentically, regardless of any judgment, fear, or intimidation you may encounter. He created your signature qualities not only to influence your life but also to impact the world. It's important to be yourself, believe in yourself, and stay true to yourself. If you suppress your voice, you undermine a significant part of who you are. Over time, it may prove to be one of your biggest regrets.

SIGNATURE SELF-TALK

In the thought-provoking book *The Top Five Regrets of the Dying*, Bronnie Ware, an Australian hospice nurse, shares her eye-opening experiences with her beloved patients. She explains how her life was transformed by what she heard during their final days and last breaths. The top regret expressed was, "I wish I'd had the courage to live a life true to myself, not the life others expected of me."[5] Also on the top five list was, "I wish I'd had the courage to express my feelings."[6] In their last moments, many of Ware's patients recognized the detriment of being unable to influence *themselves* to do what they yearned to do. They felt the pain of missing out on living the way they wanted to live, but now it was too late. They sacrificed their voice, their desires, and the authentic life they had hoped to live.

It was an epic wake-up call for me to read how each person felt such a sense of personal loss. As they approached their death and final assessment of how they had lived their life, they finally saw a clear picture of what mattered and what did not. Their minds weighed heavily with what they had *lost* as opposed to what they had *gained*. As uncomfortable and painful as it was, it became the time to recount their life and face their deepest regrets. As it has been so profoundly put, ask the *dying* if you want to understand more about *living*.

Although it is ultimately your choice to allow any outside influence to suppress you, you may feel like your authentic voice has been slipping. You may have struggled to separate and appreciate your own voice. You may know in your heart that you have lost the essence of who you are in how you speak. If you have given up your authority over your voice or are so highly influenced by others that it feels faint, it's time to regain control. God has given you specific authority that is yours alone to speak from, both to yourself and to the world. How can you stand in that powerful God-given authority if you are not entirely controlling your voice and influence?

When you take command, your voice will begin to align with who you are on the inside. It's not about becoming overly brazen or loud; it's about ensuring that prominent voices around you are not dominating who you are and the person God designed you to be. "For God has not given us a spirit of fear, but of power and of love and of a sound mind" (2 Timothy 1:7 NKJV). You have everything you need to shine in your signature style and always be your authentic self.

AUDITING DAILY INFLUENCES

In this chapter, we've talked about taking charge of the influence in us and around us. So how do we begin to audit our daily influences when we are saturated in live footage of world chaos and destruction twenty-four hours a day? Along with the information age comes the norm of seeing graphic and often shocking details of events unfolding near and far. Streams of extreme violence, gore, and catastrophic events can appear in our news feed anytime without warning. It pulsates through our culture at an alarming speed. If we are not careful, it can begin to weigh down our thinking and escalate our fear. As the burden of reality intensifies in our minds, a growing number of people are being overcome, lost, and overwhelmed by it. God wants us to know how to handle it and what to do. He wants us to have the self-control and ability to *influence our self-talk* and live wisely. He knows the battle we face, both *in* our minds and *for* our minds.

If we zoom in closer to home to snap a picture on any busy city street, we will undoubtedly catch a glimpse of current culture. Many people are either absorbed in a screen display, tuned into their earbuds, or engaged in conversation on their cell phones. They search, scroll, watch, listen, and read into oblivion. Their little devices serve as a comfort, a companion, and an enticing gateway to connect with the world. The emotional pull of curiosity to check the minute-by-minute developments in the news or in the lives of others is too much to resist. It can become a habit, an obsession, and, soon, a lifestyle that controls us rather than us controlling it. But we must admit that it's much more than an intriguing source that entertains, educates, inspires, or helps us socialize or even shop. It's a magnetic source of *influence* in our life.

What fights for *your* time every day? Whose voices sit waiting and ready to compete for your attention? With distractions at an all-time high, it can take a lot more to grab your *own* attention these days. Knowing how to rise above the mass amount of noise and opinions is critical as information overload escalates. To truly achieve the life we desire, we must separate our voices from the pack. Just as important, we also must prioritize how we guard our minds against the impressions bombarding us daily.

I know it's easy to want to ignore the responsibility of managing our daily influences. Still, only we can control the noise we allow around us. What we read, what we watch, and whom we listen to add up to a cascade of influence that targets our minds and emotions. Like sparking a wildfire, it can start to spread out of control. We can be swallowed up in a whirlwind of "content clutter" that is overwhelming. In the simple act of exposing ourselves to it, we extend permission for it to enter our thinking. Most concerning, we may not know what is actually getting in and how it is affecting us.

All day long, the conscious and unconscious parts of our mind stay busy absorbing information that can influence and alter our thinking. It's never been more important to choose our influences and surroundings well. At any moment, millions of things are waiting in the wings to hijack our thoughts. One distraction turns into many, and a minute turns into an hour. In one way or another, we will end up paying the price for how we are spending and investing our time and our attention each day.

Instead of drifting into what can numb our sensibilities, we need to sharpen our own influence over ourselves. God provides every tool we need to stand firm and resist the darkness and pressure of the world around us. He can build us up from the inside. Regardless of the rising level of noise and distraction around us, God will give us exactly what we need to influence ourselves. But it's up to us to *use* it.

We go to great lengths to fiercely protect the ones we love, yet how often do we forget to protect ourselves? It's paramount that we are intentional, not impressionable. Specific, not scattered. Delivered, not deceived. No one else can manage our ear gate, our eye gate, and our mind gate. God has entrusted us with these all-important decisions. Who's winning in the war of influence in your mind?

TAKING CONTROL OF INFLUENCES

As you can see, there are endless sources that can deeply move you and impact your life, sometimes without you even being aware. Yet there is still only one commanding influence in your life that has the *ability* and the *authority* to supersede them all. It is the God-given influence you hold over *yourself.* Indeed, the *development* of your life-changing individual influence deserves your time, effort, and careful attention every day.

One of the best places to start upgrading your thought game is to examine what surrounds you in your daily routine. Take inventory of what is currently influencing you. When you take an honest look into how each one affects your life, you can decide what changes need to be made. You can begin to reshape your life by altering your influences at any time.

For a starting point to evaluate your present influences, take a sheet of paper and put a line down the middle. On one side, list the people, places, and things that genuinely benefit your mind, body, and spirit. They strengthen and build you up and promote a closer relationship with God. On the other side, list your poor influences, the sources that always seem to weaken and drain you. They steal your peace and often lead to a spiral in your thoughts. Whether it's certain people, social media, the news, or other daily routines that meddle in your thoughts and moods, honestly analyze how they affect and influence you. This is a decisive first step toward taking control. When you take command to identify and start cutting off any sources that feed stressful, tempting, harmful, distracting, time-wasting, and destructive effects, you are putting your influence and authority into action!

You get to carefully weigh and evaluate the impact every voice, including your own, will have on you. You are 100 percent in charge of the approval process. You can regulate your influence by carefully choosing what you *will* and *will not* allow in your life. You control whom you turn up, turn down, edit, or delete.

REVOLUTIONIZE SELF-FULFILLING PROPHECIES

If you're familiar with how a self-fulfilling prophecy works, you know that what you *think, believe,* and *say* is often literally what you will get. Good or bad, what you expect to happen usually shows up. If you feel you're not good enough or you can't do something, your thoughts, beliefs, and actions will usually follow right in line with that thinking. But when you think you're intelligent and worthy and believe in your capabilities, it fires up a completely *different* set of feelings, beliefs, and actions. Is it any wonder that we must carefully weigh our words and watch how we think? What may seem like an innocent thought can be the spark that starts an entire inferno! The bottom line is that we constantly prove ourselves correct, which can, once again, either work *for* us or *against* us.

Your signature influence can do more heavy lifting than you may realize. You can dramatically change your end results when you start by aiming for the *correct* targets. Not just in what you *think* but also in what you *believe* and *say*. No matter how a situation may feel or appear, embolden your faith and get into a habit and pattern of setting high expectations and always predicting best-case scenarios. With that kind of discerning mindset, you will not only look for but *welcome* your self-fulfilling prophecies.

BUILDING INTEGRITY AND SELF-TRUST

You build your integrity every time you influence yourself for good, positive, worthwhile things. You are proving yourself *to* yourself whenever you follow through with personal action, a promise, or a commitment. It's in the small everyday things that come out when no one is looking but *you*. It may be for your eyes only, but it still influences your life.

Your *actions* keep building and strengthening the *authority* of your own word and intentions. If you tell yourself, "I'm going to do a thirty-minute aerobic workout today," and you honor that, you build trust in yourself. If you tell yourself, "I'm not going to be late for that meeting again," and then you are, you lose a little trust. When you let your yes be yes and your no be no *to yourself*, you are building your *self-influence*. Little by little, the stronger that muscle becomes to trust yourself, the more it will flow into every part of your life. It's imperative to keep exercising, building, and strengthening your level of self-trust every day.

Even when you are tested by intense adversity, you can learn more about yourself as every part of you shows up to push through it. You can see how genuinely faithful, reliable, and capable you are. As uncomfortable as it may be, this rocky terrain will build up more strength and instill even higher levels of self-trust.

So, the moment of truth. What is your current state of influencing and trusting yourself? Do you trust your ability to draw upon God's strength and power and handle anything that could come your way? If not, where does that leave you if you don't believe in yourself or trust your own abilities?

When you stay close to God and spend time getting to know yourself better than ever before, your signature influence will soar. You will understand how to rule your behavior, potential, and authentic voice. As you grow more confident in these areas, it will revolutionize your self-fulfilling prophecies and build your integrity and self-trust. It is a process of creating a life where you continue to excel in meaning, purpose, and impact. Most of all, without regret, you will stand firm in living a life true to yourself, not based on what others expect of you.

In the next chapter, we move into another critical area of self-influence, strengthening your ability to encourage yourself!

Chapter 5

ENCOURAGING YOURSELF

It wasn't a dream or a wild hallucination. I blinked again as I turned to see that it really was my mom flying the plane! Instead of our usual visit over coffee, here we were, high in the sky, laughing and casually chatting in the cockpit of a small private airplane. As I glanced out the window, my mind suddenly flashed back to all the milestones that led to this moment. Mom's long-held dream of becoming a pilot had occasionally popped up in conversation over the years. But it wasn't until she was in her fifties, after a busy life and raising five kids, that the opportunity *unexpectedly* arrived.

My dad, who loved supporting my mom in her dreams, was thrilled to surprise her with an extra special gift he had secretly arranged one year. He bought her a pricey membership in a flying club, and she was all set to take lessons to finally become a private pilot. The only problem was, Dad didn't realize things had shifted with Mom's aviation dreams over the years. She had never mentioned it, but she had actually developed problems with air sickness and a fear of flying! To make matters even worse, the money spent on the membership was nonrefundable. Mom was so touched by the grand gesture that she didn't say a word but decided to press forward.

The flight instructor was a pastor in town, which helped to put Mom more at ease. It was indeed a plus for all the praying going on. Aside from overcoming her fears, she embarked on a steep learning curve that was not easy. She encouraged herself to keep going step by step as she progressed from ground school to in-air flight lessons and eventually to the arduous written exam. Finally, after many months of extensive training, it came time for her last test required to obtain her private pilot's license: a solo cross-country flight. She would be required to execute all aspects of a five-and-a-half-hour flight involving checkpoints at three different airports and traveling more than 150 nautical miles. Her first solo trip would test not only her aviation knowledge but also her focus, inner strength, and courage.

Although it was enormously stressful and Mom had some nerve-wracking moments on that first trip alone, she was not shaken. She trusted God to help her influence her thoughts to stay on track. It was a monumental test of strength under pressure, and she passed it, inside and out. She stepped out in faith, faced every obstacle, and despite her initial fears, she pressed on to finally achieve her lifelong dream of becoming a private pilot.

And now we were ten thousand feet in the air after she had conquered it all. Sitting beside her in silent admiration, I couldn't help but think, "Wow, that's my mom flying this plane!"

FLYING SOLO IN LIFE

We will all have instances in life when we seem to be flying solo. It may be a matter of being physically alone, but it could also be a feeling of being on our own in the world. These times will be the actual test of how we either know or don't know how to encourage *ourselves*.

Are you comfortable being alone with nothing more than you and your own thoughts? What happens to you in those mundane gaps between work, conversations, screen time, and TV shows? How do you feel when you are left alone in those stark moments? It may seem silly, but it's a question many people don't want to face. No matter how much you can fill up your time by staying busy or making the rounds to check for updates on all your devices, you will still have times when you are left with the quiet presence of just being with *you*. Thinking, feeling, breathing, wonderful *you*. How do you handle it? Do those times alone seem awkward? You can do everything possible to rush past them or grab for anything that will relieve the feeling of being alone. But no matter how you try to ignore or push those moments aside, they will always be part of life. Instead, I want to help you not only be content in your own company but get really good at using those times to your full advantage. I want you to see that there is great value in being comfortable being alone.

Whenever we feel like we are flying solo in life, especially in crisis moments, God can help us show up boldly for ourselves. He moves in us so we can move into how we need to think, decide, and take action. In other words, God speaks to and influences us so we can influence ourselves. We can become highly skilled at reacting better and faster in *any* situation when we understand how to effectively encourage *ourselves*. The more we practice it in our everyday life, the better it prepares us to show up for ourselves in high-pressure times.

ENCOURAGING YOURSELF THROUGH ADVERSITY

I remember a few white-knuckle moments myself when I cried out to God. In every one of them, He helped me to not panic but encourage myself through it, moment by shaky moment. I will never forget being stuck in traffic on a burning mountain pass or the time I was driving on slippery roads in a late-night snowstorm and thick fog. On another occasion, I endured the shock of a severe earthquake in the middle of the night, and another time, I experienced a sense of deep overwhelm when I missed a flight and was stranded in a foreign country. I faced all these situations (pre-cell phones, I might add) and much more *alone*. It was God and me. He was right there regardless of how dangerous or scary the problem appeared. It always amazed me that when I turned to Him, it not only altered how I processed the struggle *inside* but also changed how I stepped into handling the problem *outside*. It became much more than simply passing a test of faith. It was developing deep roots of knowing how to *use* God's power in me to *encourage myself* forward.

We can never underestimate how the wretched challenges in life strengthen us and allow us to hone some invaluable skills. Trying circumstances can sharpen what was dull. Unexpected challenges can refine and enrich rough areas. Our minds can be opened to new insights that can forever change how we will react in the future.

Beyond any doubt, it's not easy to have a sudden crash course that can test us to the core. But the results can serve a genuinely high purpose. In my own life and many others, it is astonishing to see how God can use a trial in a *season* to produce essential skills for a *lifetime*.

The ability to encourage yourself in your darkest times can be priceless. If you've been through some deep struggles, you understand being put in a position where you've had to force yourself to keep going. There was no choice but to find ways to encourage yourself to make it through to the other side. You had to dig deeper, try harder, get creative, and discover places inside you that some people will never come close to tapping into. Every day your feet hit the floor, you strengthened that forward muscle.

Imagine if life was always smooth with no bumps in the road. Would you have ever developed the traits that have now proven to be some of your greatest strengths? Most likely you would have only skimmed the surface of what you really have inside you. In every adversity you've faced, even in bitter suffering that was so difficult to understand at the time, be assured that you didn't become *less*; you became *more*.

ENCOURAGING YOURSELF IN LONELINESS AND ISOLATION

For some people, their greatest fear is being alone. There's just something about painfully quiet moments with nowhere to go, nothing to do, and no one around. It can seem not only uncomfortable but like a total waste of time to be left with nothing but their own thoughts. It can trigger a reaction of wanting to be anywhere but sitting alone. Do you ever feel that way? Although being alone will inevitably be a part of our life experience at times, many lack the basic skills to cope with it. One of the most challenging tests of encouraging ourselves can come into play when we face isolation or loneliness.

Earlier in life, when I was singing professionally, I lived and worked for some time in Japan and experienced their fascinating culture. More than just a beautiful country, Japan is known to have the oldest population in the entire world. Although they believe that living longer is a great blessing, some rather unusual problems have developed out of the loneliness it can bring. Instead of learning to encourage themselves, some senior women are willing to pay a high price to escape their painful moments alone. In fact, they have even been willing to give up their precious freedom.

According to a 2018 article in *Bloomberg Businessweek* entitled "Japan's Prisons Are a Haven for Elderly Women," older women in Japan have been *purposely* committing petty theft crimes so they will be put in jail.[7] They prefer to be locked up where they can feel a part of a community and have someone to talk to. Surprisingly, this escape from a lonely life has become an even bigger problem. They don't want to leave! They are willing to trade their freedom to stay connected with other women.

With these ongoing issues, Japan has stepped up its efforts to help battle deep loneliness. One solution was developing a series of companion robots to keep people company.[8] These AI creatures can actually hold conversations and provide support. Remarkably, these life-like robots can react to human emotions and give a sense of feeling loved.

Mechanical friends can resemble pets or be a mirror image of a human-looking woman. They have even produced a polar bear figure to carry patients around and provide elderly care. These creations are designed to step into the role of providing social engagement, positive mood boosters, and friendly company. It's a unique concept to help with the ongoing struggles of those battling loneliness and disconnection.

Even before the 2020 pandemic hit, numerous surveys and studies in recent years have shown a US national decline in friendships and devastating levels of loneliness and social isolation.[9] Where it was once thought that mostly older people faced these painful conditions, it has now been determined that they affect more than the elderly. Now people of all ages and stages of life are dealing with a profound sense of loss and loneliness.

ENCOURAGING YOURSELF IN ALL CIRCUMSTANCES

Many of us have experienced losing our way in connecting with *ourselves*. We can ignore our inner world for so long that we practically become invisible to ourselves. We must stay in touch with our ability to motivate, entertain, encourage, and influence ourselves into action. Yes, God designed us for connection, companionship, and community. However, we can never forget what He has placed inside us to *use* and *enjoy*, *e*specially when we are alone. We never know if our circumstances may change ahead or when our family and social circles could shift. Whatever life brings, God wants us always to see the importance of being able to encourage ourselves as well.

God knows what you have ahead and who will and won't be there to share in it. He also knows what you need to encourage yourself right now and to handle what's down the road. The Lord has *already* planned for all those times when there may be no one to help you, support you, cheer you on, or even pay attention. Regardless, He will faithfully provide and be there to continue to work on the inside of you, to rev up His power *in* you and *for* you, so you can keep going. Beyond anything the world could ever give, *His* inner strength at work within you is unfailing—not only to help you stand in faith but to fire up your ability to encourage *yourself* in every circumstance.

As we've discovered with recent world changes, it has become more critical than ever to develop the ability to stand firm and thrive, behind closed doors, during *any* period of isolation. You *can* lean into and even learn to embrace times alone. Silence does not have to be deafening. In fact, God does some of His best work when we have slowed down and entered into greater stillness. It's the prime condition for incredible transformation to take shape. Greater clarity and creativity can surface, our character can be strengthened, and new dreams and visions can come alive. Time alone can be vital to accelerating our growth and unlocking new ideas. It starts by believing and trusting that God can use the time apart to make us stronger, wiser, and more powerful. It can also prepare us to accomplish the incredible things He has for us in the future.

ENCOURAGING YOURSELF NOT TO GIVE UP
Everyday stories and real-life examples of unusually courageous people inspire us. We applaud and admire their actions and can be left speechless by their incredible stories. It's difficult to wrap our minds around what they went through, from experiencing a full-blown crisis to suffering inconceivable loss. Yet somehow, they beat unthinkable odds. They miraculously survived what would have crippled so many others. We lean in, wanting to know more about their personal experience. How did they speak to themselves amid the chaos? How did they talk to God? When there was no foreseeable end in sight, we are curious how they could encourage themselves to keep going and *not* give up.

In facing the unexpected in life, there may be times when we need to encourage ourselves through a time of crisis that can last hours or days. In his book *Alone: Lost Overboard in the Indian Ocean,* Brett Archibald recounts the ordeal that forever changed his life.[10] With a rain and wind storm raging, he was getting sick over the side of a charter boat in the middle of the night. Suddenly, he lost his balance and fell overboard. His frantic screams were never heard as the vessel drifted away. Since everyone was asleep, it would be hours before they realized he was missing. Feeling sure he would die, he entered into a desperate conversation with God. But surprisingly, what started out in anger soon made a turn. He began to sing, recite facts and information, and do everything possible to keep his mind alert and engaged. He continued to tread water for seemingly endless hours. Even though he had moments of fearing his life was over, he just kept going. Somehow, he kept thinking and moving until help finally arrived to rescue him—twenty-eight hours later! God miraculously filled him with what he needed to encourage himself.

What about more extended challenges in life where painful circumstances can go on for many months? That's when we must encourage ourselves to withstand both pressure and the test of time. In 1945 my Uncle Neal, one of my heroes in life, faced the grave reality of being a prisoner of war. Captured and held for seven long months in a prisoner camp, he endured torture and trauma that were shocking. Although unable to talk about it for many years, my uncle eventually shared more about the excruciating experience and the horrendous conditions he was forced to bear. He lost sixty pounds due to the brutal labor work camp and starvation. If he dared to fall in weakness, he would have been shot. Despite being uncertain if he would ever return home, he never gave up. I will always be grateful for his faith, courage, and sacrifice but, even more, for how he pressed into God and chose to fiercely encourage himself forward.

Sometimes, even more demanding than several months, we may have to keep encouraging ourselves for many *years*. In Athens, Greece, in 2004, Olympic hopeful Ruth Beitia, a six-foot-three high jump contender, entered the arena to compete for a medal. She took sixteenth place in the event but didn't stop there. In Beijing in 2008, she returned to try again and took fourth place. Still encouraging herself to keep going, she competed in London in 2012 and once again placed fourth. Disappointed but deciding she would not give up, Ruth decided against retiring, and she trained hard to try one more time at the 2016 Olympics in Rio de Janeiro.

After *twelve* long years, she entered the arena for her fourth try. She finally achieved first place, won the gold medal, and even made history as the oldest champion in a high jump event! Far beyond her impressive victory was her unwavering journey to earning it. Ruth was a real-life example of persistence in breaking through every failure, disappointment, and the temptation to give up. When most would have quit, she passionately encouraged herself to keep going, no matter what, year after year.[11]

> "I was found by people who were not looking for me.
> I showed myself to those who were not
> asking for me."
> —Romans 10:20 NLT

MIRACULOUS ENCOURAGEMENT

As stories of utter miracles continue to touch our lives and shake up our thinking, we see how God can shine a light on His goodness in the world. He continues to encourage us and strengthen our faith through the wondrous things we see and hear and even in what we experience ourselves. These events not only deepen our faith in God but reinforce that nothing, absolutely nothing, is impossible with Him. From miraculous stories involving plane crashes and tragic car accidents to natural disasters where no one should have survived, it is stunning to see how God made a way where there was no logical way. The *way* He created was not only in outer circumstances but also in what He accomplished *inside* people so they would not give up. In every second of the emergency, while waiting for help, they somehow found the strength to encourage themselves to hang on in those devastating moments. Only they and God will ever know how they spoke to themselves, over and over, to generate the incredible mental stamina needed for hours, days, months, or even years. We can only assume that it must have been a genuinely *miraculous* kind of self-talk.

> **"I am the LORD; there is no other God.
> I will give you the strength you need, although you do not know me."
> —Isaiah 45:5 GNT**

Whether it is a crisis, ongoing suffering, or a delayed dream, we will never know all the people walking around this world who have encouraged themselves through unthinkable conditions. Some will confess that God gave them the hope and strength to keep going. He did what they could not do on their own. They endured enormous inner battles, yet they were able to hold on and keep encouraging themselves forward. Their faith went into action with specific self-talk that sustained them. In those dire moments, alone and afraid, they set the right thoughts in motion. Each of them had to *choose* to encourage and *keep* encouraging *themselves*.

The point is that you, too, can rally and encourage yourself through *any* of your life circumstances. God wants you to know how to strengthen your faith and stand unwavering. Whether it's an urgent, devastating problem or an ongoing battle, you will always be faced with the choice either to encourage yourself or to give up. Moment by moment, you alone have to put your faith into action and choose the direction of your *thinking*. Although we never know what to expect every day, we should remember this vital principle. Whatever we practice in the *ordinary* course of life will surface in the *extraordinary* events of life.

> "God is our refuge and strength, an
> ever-present help in trouble."
> —Psalm 46:1 NIV

THE COURAGE BANK
In this chapter, we've talked about encouraging ourselves through harsh and uncomfortable adversities in life. When our courage is stirred, and we move into brave action, these experiences become a part of our life stories. I look at each one as a *deposit* into what I call our personal "courage account." Our deposits may start small, but like a tiny spark that starts a blazing fire, our courage can spread quickly. It can ignite our confidence, unleash our creativity, accelerate personal growth, and generate phenomenal success.

Our courage plays a crucial role in how we handle every one of our career, business, and life decisions. In fact, it can lead us to level up in *everything* we do. Is it any wonder God directs us to be strong and courageous? Our courage, or lack thereof, is often the one giant hurdle between us and the great things He wants us to accomplish.

I can't help but marvel at how some people are zealous about testing their courage. Whether running a daunting marathon, braving a dramatic bungee jump, scaling a rugged mountain, or skydiving out of a plane. What they do may play out physically, but it also reveals what they can withstand mentally and emotionally. They seem to have a burning desire to take risks, confront danger head-on, and endure pain, even when they don't have to! It's entirely their own choice, and they do it boldly and willingly. Deep down, they have a personal motive for pushing themselves to go above and beyond what most people would. They embrace the chance to enlarge their limits and prove something to *themselves*. When they finally meet the moment and succeed at their mission, they know they have achieved a payoff that no one else may ever fully understand. It's as if each victory is a gold nugget that goes into their treasure chest of life.

Although most of us will never be driven toward the extreme in our acts of courage, every one of us will make deposits into our courage account. In big and small ways, we will make substantial deposits from our own brave acts and the storms we have weathered in life. As time goes on, those deposits keep building and growing. Best of all, they are there to draw upon anytime we need them—today, tomorrow, or even decades in the future. Through the miracle of compounding, our courage multiplies and keeps producing so it can be used to keep doing more and becoming more over time. The earlier we get started, the more we can grow our courage and use it in every area of our lives. This account is not only a sound investment, but the returns are off the charts!

I will be forever grateful to have started making considerable courage deposits at a young age. In fact, the experiences I have banked over the years continue to influence me today. They are indeed the gift that keeps on giving! My courage account contains a record of the difficulties I've overcome and the goals I've achieved. Most importantly, it holds the testimonies of God's utter faithfulness that got me through every stressful, messy, chaotic, and crazy moment. In fact, if it had not been for the solid *proof* of my grit sitting in that account, I may not have mustered the courage needed to acquire and run a staffing company solely on my own. What I saw in my history in that account made all the difference in convincing me of what I could do and the pressure I could withstand. It was *fuel* for my faith. Courage breeds courage.

The many deeds stashed away in that secret place are my treasure chest. More precious than gold or silver, it is filled with my life experiences that are carefully preserved and prominently stamped with four decisive words: "In God I trust!" Until my last breath, I will keep building, depositing, withdrawing, and actively using my courage account to navigate life. No matter how God calls me to be strong and courageous in the future, I will continue to pull from the riches He has given me that are safely stored away, yet never forgotten, in my priceless "courage account."

> "But then I recall all you have done, O Lord;
> I remember your wonderful deeds of long ago.
> They are constantly in my thoughts. I cannot stop
> thinking about your mighty works."
> —**Psalm 77:11–12 NLT**

BUILDING YOUR COURAGE ACCOUNT

So, let me ask you a question. Are you capitalizing on your courageous life stories and using them to their *full* potential? Have you been highlighting or burying your brave moments? Imagine how you might approach life with a new boost of courage if you were to tally up your own remarkable history. Think of all you have done and overcome that required absolute fortitude. Decide today to start your list and get some deposits on record for your own courage account. That secret stash can be used in mighty ways when you get your mind *fixed* on your courageous feats and all God has brought you through. Own your courage. It can become fire and fuel when you use where you have *been* to strengthen where you are *going*.

Every time you put your faith into definitive action, your experiences are deposited in your heart, mind, and soul. They also deserve a prime place in your memory bank for the crusades ahead. What you honor from your past can help you embrace the future. When you are forty and worried about shifting careers, draw upon the unbelievable determination you had in your twenties when you were pushing through high-stress decisions. Yes, that was you. You did it before and will do it again, even better! When you are seventy and start questioning what you can still contribute to the world, look back on the guts you had in your fifties when you fired up your creativity and launched a new venture. That grit is still a part of who you are. Whenever you face a transition, remember how you conquered tricky changes in the past. If you suffer a painful loss, remember how you coped with loss before, and be assured that God will see you through it again. In every circumstance that life throws you, tell yourself boldly and relentlessly, "My faith and courage have been built for this!"

Only you know all the times that triggered your courage and what you did that took guts. Think about the stockpile of internal evidence you hold just waiting to show you how capable you are. Keep activating those positive assets—*feeling* them, *thinking* about them, and *using* them. As life goes on, you will accumulate a wealth of courage in your account that's yours alone to use. But only you can access all of this abundance. To unlock it, you simply have to *remember* it and *use* it. Now and forever, it stands ready and able to help you be courageous in facing your past, present, and future. You draw off of your mighty account whenever you play the stories in your mind of what God has done *in* you, *for* you, and *through* you. In fact, this is how you keep filling yourself with greater and greater courage, also known as . . . *encouraging yourself*!

In an ever-changing and uncertain world, you know that there will most definitely be times ahead when you will need a substantial supply of courage and the innate ability to encourage yourself. Instead of being anxious about the unknown around the corner, use your thoughts wisely to be resourceful and well prepared inside. There has never been a better time to build more courage *reserves* and keep using your personal currency to stand firm and courageous in everything you do. Whether flying solo through hardship, loneliness, or unique challenges, the most significant and life-changing work you can do is *within*. When you meet God in that secret place, in good times or bad, He will empower you to encourage yourself.

Next, let's look at how you can upgrade your inner game as we dive into how you can build more *internal* assets and prepare yourself for greater success!

Chapter 6

PREPARING FOR TRANSFORMATION

If you've ever watched the movie *Rocky*, you have seen how the dream and conviction of a simple man is ignited into unbeatable strength. He defies all the odds to become a champion fighter. His is a story of heart, extraordinary drive, determination, and a hunger for victory.

As Rocky Balboa steps into action to train, he progressively pushes himself harder. He grows stronger mentally and physically, transforming his body, mind, and spirit into who he needs to be to win. All of the grueling preparation is finally put to the test when he steps into the ring to face his powerful opponent. At first, he appears to be taking a horrible beating. It's painful to watch as he continues to go down and seems to be heading straight for defeat. But suddenly, as if a switch is flipped on, you see that something inside him drastically shifts. He rises to his feet to make it clear that he is *not* staying down. The crowd goes wild, watching in shock as he moves in a sudden surge of strength to pour out everything he has. Unexpectedly, he takes back control to win an explosive victory!

TRANSFORMATION STARTS WITH INNER PREPARATION

Like for Rocky, one of the most challenging and soul-consuming battles we can face is the struggle of getting from the individual we are to the person we would like to be. Where do we start when everything in us wants to achieve a goal? How do we prepare when we face unfamiliar territory or a formidable new challenge? If we truly believe something will happen, we should *prepare* for it.

It's one thing to think God *can* do something in and for us. But it's a whole new level of faith to believe God *will*. We *will* get ready if we fully trust that He will do what He says He will do, whether we are thinking of getting a new job, being healed in a particular area, having a long-awaited baby, or any other similar endeavor. When we genuinely expect something to occur, we spend time thinking about it and planning for it to happen. We get all the little details in place to be ready to receive it, and we start to get excited about it! What will you be well-prepared to have, do, become, or achieve?

This is a time for our story to expand and for new chapters to be written. We must move in strength and power to conquer giants and gain new ground. The question is, are we well prepared? Preparation is a significant but easily overlooked part of our faith. While many of us will say we believe, do we actually do much to prepare? Do we begin to align our thinking and our lives to receive what we've asked God for? How often do we honestly *prepare* for big doors of blessing to open and our big prayers to be answered?

PREPARING FOR TRANSFORMATION

It's essential to look at how we prepare *now* if we've desired phenomenal success in our finances, career, relationships, and lives in the *future*. A good starting point is to not allow your everyday life to keep you so focused on what you're going to *do* that you miss entirely thinking about what you're going to *be*. Like Rocky's small beginnings, focusing on what you want to *become* will inevitably affect what you *do*. They are interconnected. You must get the correct thinking in motion daily if you want to accelerate your desired changes. Most people are not born with an iron will, natural strength, or a zealous driving force. These have to be developed. Your signature self-talk can become the course of action to help you build those characteristics. Gaining better control over yourself and your habits leads to more decisive thinking and vigorous living.

Big or small, every goal involves a transformation of some kind. An inevitable beginning and an end, a before and an after, and a process in between. Just like the simple "dash" mark on a headstone in the cemetery representing *everything* between life and death, we can never forget that what happens in the *middle* truly matters.

If we break it down to the bare basics, a transformation goes from point A to point B. Every time there is a space between where you are now and where you want to be, you've got two predetermined points. Learning to insert and activate an effective self-talk strategy in that middle ground will help get you there faster and more successfully every time. Your self-talk is critical to carry you between those two points. It will influence and fuel you in this crucial middle ground. Usually, gaps exist between what you're doing *now* and what you *want* to be doing. Whether it is a specific change you want in your personal life or a defined goal in your career or business, you need an excellent self-talk strategy and a winning belief system from start to finish. Both the *substance* and *strength* of your self-talk, positive or negative, will determine the outcomes of your point-A-to-point-B journeys.

> **"That is the way I run, with a clear goal in mind. That is the way I fight, not like someone shadow boxing."**
> **—1 Corinthians 9:26 ISV**

DEVELOPING A WINNING BELIEF SYSTEM

How often have you felt as if you were thriving in one season and barely surviving in another? Although you can feel empowered and accomplished in the high times, you might hit a low point at other times and feel like you can't get anything right. You may be a leader and top performer one year and completely lose your footing the following year. Think of all the series of changes that have occurred in your life. Your intense highs and disappointing lows. Your wins and losses. Not only with outside circumstances but shifts in your body, mind, and emotions. How did you think of yourself, look at yourself, and talk to or treat yourself *differently* when you hit the high points in your life? How about the low times? This endless challenge creates the need for a faith-driven belief system in both *God* and *yourself* that will endure *all of* life's ups and downs. Not just to handle change but to navigate it *well*.

You must develop a winning belief system to overcome your challenges and succeed. Regardless of who else may believe in you, *y*our own mind needs to be fully persuaded to believe. Not only persuaded about what you think of yourself but thoroughly convinced of what you can do. Like in *Rocky*, your actions will follow your beliefs, no matter what you face. You act according to the things you say and *believe*.

Never underestimate how much your own self-talk can awaken your imagination. It can help you envision higher levels of yourself, whatever that looks like. What God can do in and through you is without measure. In fact, what can seem impossible one day may not seem impossible at all the next day. Your self-talk is key to validating your ideas and drumming up the confidence to take those ideas to the next step. When you are mentally savvy, you stay engaged and hold tightly to possibility and the conviction to make your dreams a reality. Think of all the profitable ideas, fresh perspectives, exciting innovations, and life-altering inventions that may exist in you. You have *signature creations* waiting to be introduced to the world. God plants and *keeps* planting excellence inside you so you will flourish. You only need the winning belief system in Him and in yourself to *use* what He gives you to create an extraordinary life.

Each person's blend of talents creates his or her own signature style of self-expression with everything they design and produce. Consider how great stories are written, brilliant ideas developed, color takes shape on a canvas, and music forms into an unforgettable song. God-given talents spring to life from the inside out. History continues to prove that the human imagination has no limits. Every invention can trace back to an idea that started *inside* a person. From there it blossomed into form with a robust *belief system* fueling it, from the first airplane clumsily leaving the ground to the mind-bending computer age. Deep down, those who introduced new concepts had to *believe* it was possible. They trusted their own instincts and invested tremendous time and effort. Even more, releasing their novel idea into the world took *guts*. Can you imagine where we would be and what our world would look like today had they never dared to take that chance?

Unchartered territory continues to stretch the imagination every day. The limits of human knowledge and unbridled creativity will constantly be tested. Life's mysteries will trigger new ideas, discoveries, and unheard-of solutions to break even greater ground ahead. With a winning belief system, we can hold to the promise that with God, *nothing* is impossible! Nothing is impossible in the world, and nothing is impossible in our lives.

How solid is your belief system in what *you* can do, have, and become? Remember how the self-talk affected the jumpers on the ten-meter platform? Your self-talk can be the spark to talk you *into* or *out of* what to believe. When you feel weak, insecure, or discouraged, it is not easy to envision your success ahead. But when you take the reins of what you say to yourself, you can start refining your inner world. You can begin to act *on purpose* to adjust and ignite your own set of beliefs as you pay more attention to following your best voice and instincts.

It's exhilarating to take hold of the actual force your signature self-talk can be. You learn to sort positive and negative thoughts quickly, by pure intention. You can then skillfully *design* and *align* better self-talk to reinforce what you decide is the right way to believe. You can choose to operate in a winning belief system that conveys profitable messages to your own mind. Streaming your own influence over your thought life every day is empowering!

THE DOMINO EFFECT OF SELF-TALK

Your self-talk is that monumental *first* domino that sets off a subsequent chain reaction in every detail of your life. It is the dynamo agent to start, stop, and effect change in each area. You alone determine if your self-talk will be your greatest friend or worst enemy. Whether you will use it to lift you up or allow it to crush you down is your decision. Most people beat themselves up more than anybody else ever could. Even worse, for some people, the most toxic of all their relationships can be with *themselves*, especially in times of failure. This is why we are on this mission to influence *ourselves* with *life-building* self-talk.

Have you ever considered your self-talk as the underlying force and common denominator in all your "self" components? How is your *self-talk* impacting your self-motivation, self-discipline, self-control, self-confidence, and self-improvement? It is your *own* dialogue that is setting off the all-powerful first domino and striking everything that follows after it. One negative thought can lead to another and another. But on the flip side, one positive thought can certainly multiply our thinking in a *good* direction. God's incredible wisdom tells us to take every thought captive and get it headed in the *right* direction. It only takes one thought to quickly start forming a pattern.

Getting your self-talk right will affect every detail of your life and how you show up for *yourself*. It is the make-or-break factor in your health and happiness, work and achievements, and overall success. When you position that first domino in the *right* way, it can set off a promising chain reaction that leads to positive results. Getting that first domino right affects the whole pattern and how everything falls. It is cause for celebration when you understand how to continually set the best elements in motion to produce a reliable self-talk arsenal.

As many at the top of their game will testify, strategically setting up their self-talk has helped them shift to what they *now* believe about themselves. A new world can open up as you understand how to create your own personal self-talk plan. Sure, it takes focus and effort to tailor your words and messages to yourself, but what you develop will keep growing and multiplying beyond what you can imagine. Every time you have a victory, you'll become better able to do it again and go even further the next time. Like a domino, your winning self-talk touches the next situation and then each new challenge further and further down the line.

Think of designing your signature self-talk as becoming your own expert innovator. You create the actual wording to talk yourself through each challenge and into triumph. When you have a signature plan firmly in place, you can shift your thinking faster and head for the exit when you land in a destructive frame of mind. After all, you can't afford to tip the dominos in the wrong direction and create more misery. Your self-talk plan is there to realign you quickly. It is capturing your thoughts, enabling self-control, and influencing you to stay grounded in your winning belief system. Both you and your self-talk will grow more potent every time you implement it.

We decide how and when we will influence ourselves to be more, do more, and have more.

UPGRADING OUR INNER GAME
Now that we better understand how profoundly our *inside* world affects everything in our *outside* world, it's time to focus on upgrading our *inner game*. We all must work on our inner strength to keep us on course and moving toward our *outer* achievements. That's why we will always need tools and a tactical action plan to stay on target. It's not a one-time fix. We are always in process. We must keep moving and adapting as we go. As life changes, we must continue to also *upgrade* our inner game to meet new challenges. Every giant we conquer *inside* directly affects how we handle the threatening giants *outside*.

At what point do you usually stop, give up, or settle where you are? Do you lay down your dreams when you face opposition or really fight for them? How often do you let go of what you were hoping for, believing for, or praying for? When everything in you and around you is falling apart, are you able to regroup quickly and keep going? How can you stand up for yourself out in the world if you can't even stand up *to* yourself when needed? Once you get a handle on the barriers between you and your success, you can begin to lay the groundwork to navigate them. When you set out to upgrade your inner game, it will take determination to let go of what is not working and bravely grab on to what can propel you forward.

In my own life, I desperately needed a "go-to" system when I hit tough times. When I was under high stress and feeling overwhelmed, it was critical to have a fast and easy process. I needed a preset plan, not something I had to search for or figure out when I was in distress. It had to speak to me profoundly and do some heavy lifting. As I developed my first series of signature self-talk messages, I had these all-important factors in mind. I was shocked at the impressive difference my signature messages made in those times of struggle. They were so effective at redirecting and managing my mind that I kept growing and expanding my self-talk messaging into more uses.

Unexpected problems and complicated situations can strike us anytime. Like a one-two punch, it often starts when something terrible happens to us. Like a domino, that triggering negative event tries to throw off our inner game. But regardless of the adversity, when your signature self-talk is in place, you will be ready for the unexpected. You will train like a champion, and you will be well prepared. You can speak up and speak boldly to yourself. Best of all, you will already know what to say, even in your weakest moments. Every time you need to step into action, you won't have to "reinvent the wheel." The key is not to hesitate but to move quickly to fight off and dismantle discouragement before it can set in. Don't wait. Timing matters as your thinking can spiral out of control fast. What a comfort it will be to have a solid "battle plan" secured, in advance, to take down and remove the mountains in your way. What a gift to have a signature self-talk arsenal and a personal strategy that always keeps you armed and ready. You will know how to build just that when you finish reading this book!

CHAMPION-LEVEL THINKING

Difficult times will come and go in the game of life, but your signature self-talk can change the speed you recover from life events. Learning to design and use it to safeguard and fortify your state of mind will give you the traction you need. You can overcome life's twists and turns when you *relentlessly* reframe and keep reframing rejection and failure. As you move through every pain and trial, be determined to *use* your self-talk to build more strength and resilience in yourself. Instead of succumbing to weakness or self-pity, shift over to the self-talk you've prepared that can help you recover quickly and recover *well*.

When we are mighty warriors, as God calls us to be, we are less prone to push ourselves around or take advantage of ourselves. It gives us the courage to dig in our heels and passionately roar against what we know is depleting us. A warrior mindset allows us to pick ourselves up and keep going as we rely on God's unfailing power as our inner core. Whether in times of success or distress, we keep our heads held high, proud of who we are and who God made us to be.

True inner strength stems from integrity, dignity, and grace. The ability to remain calm and wise in the face of a storm. We hold a standard of excellence that *we* set and come to expect of *ourselves*. We keep fighting the good fight, no matter the challenges around us. As we live true to our convictions, we pray bold prayers, tap into our gifts, and take proactive steps of faith. We speak victory into ourselves, our circumstances, and everything we do. We champion the right to be ourselves, and we embrace our God-given influence with courage.

OFFENSE VERSUS DEFENSE IN SELF-TALK

Have you ever noticed that many of the books and materials on self-talk focus only on using it as a *defense* strategy? In other words, the emphasis is on using it to curb negative chatter or toxic thinking. But I have discovered that our self-talk has the exciting potential to be used for so much more. It can be used as a phenomenal *offense* strategy. Beyond just correcting *destructive* self-talk, you can gain incredible momentum as you speak to and influence yourself with bold *constructive* self-talk.

What is the big difference between playing offense as opposed to defense? In an offensive position, *you* initiate action and make the moves. You are the one on the attack rather than being under attack. You don't run *from*; you run *toward*. In other words, you strategically cue your self-talk to go after the changes you want to make. You pursue your self-talk rather than it pursuing you. It becomes a regular practice to infuse your mind with signature messages and to keep influencing yourself precisely as you choose. You shape your own *thinking*, and therefore you shape your own *life*.

Whether you want to lose weight or become a best-selling author, you can activate your self-talk *when* and *how* you need it in order to accomplish a specific purpose or mission. Your signature self-talk can become your most incredible planning tool to take you to new levels in every area of life. When you stay on the *offense*, it becomes the most innovative way to protect yourself. With a mighty self-talk arsenal, you can handle incoming hits in life with more speed, efficiency, accuracy, and strength.

To get a better picture of offense versus defense, imagine Rocky standing in the boxing ring, trying only to *defend* himself. Visualize him spending all his energy trying to block himself from the pain of incoming strikes. His entire focus is on trying his best to shield and protect himself and simply weather the blows. How well would he have done in the fight with only a defensive strategy? Instead, he is ready to enter the ring with an offensive strategy prepared in advance. He is trained and confident in throwing powerful punches and applying specific techniques designed to attack and beat his opponent. He has a clear-cut plan and the intention to win! In fact, the more time he spends using his *offensive* moves, the less time he has to spend on defense. No wonder it is often said the best defense is a good offense. What does your strategy look like when you step into the ring of life every day? Are you more focused on defense or ready to step into some dynamic *offensive* moves?

"When opportunity comes, it's too late to prepare."
—Coach John Wooden

TRAINING FOR PEAK PERFORMANCE
Just like champions have to prepare in advance for their own success, we also have to train and prepare well for ours. Athletes don't just show up and randomly decide to jump into an event. They have to strengthen their abilities *ahead of time*. Before entering the competition, they carefully plan, prepare, and condition themselves for peak performance. Likewise, you

must proactively speak to yourself and intentionally prepare yourself spiritually, mentally, emotionally, and even physically every day. You have to take personal responsibility for igniting your own secret place inside that will generate your drive and determination. As a champion, you must push yourself to develop an extraordinary life *within*. It's how you install that electrifying inner switch that stands ready to be flipped. When everything looks hopelessly against you, that supernatural surge turns on, and you give it all you've got. You show yourself and the world: there's *no way* you are staying down!

With God on your side, you can refuse to hide your light or back away from your blessings. He designed you to accomplish great things, not to shrink down to fit anyone's mold. You control the dimmer switch on your light in the world. You can turn it up or turn it down. When you dedicate yourself to your regimen of inner growth, you're setting yourself up for high performance and champion-level thinking. The result? Your mindset will be in peak condition. You will be ready and able to give a quick response to demanding challenges. You won't avoid or retreat when God swings open a new door of opportunity. As He clears the path, removes the obstacles, and makes way for you to advance, you *will* be ready. Not only to move but to face your giants and run full force toward your purpose. Best of all, you will be well equipped to dare yourself to new levels and do bold things. Every day that you put God's strength inside you into action, you will continue to be more than a conqueror. When you stay on the offensive, you will *live* prepared!

PREPARING FOR VICTORY

So, the moment of truth. How have you been handling that gap between where you are now and the success you want? Have you taken time to think about what has been helping or hurting your move *upward?* Have you been waiting for victory or actually *preparing* for it? Can your mind conceive and believe it *before* it even happens?

The number of people earnestly paying close attention to how they think and operate in life is few. Especially in this fast-paced, overstimulated world we live in. Even smaller is the percentage of people who actually spend the time and effort to write their goals, practice visualization, and make a solid plan for success. In fact, this rare group of astute people often hunt for new tools and techniques that could increase their odds of high achievement. They *actively* search for and often find the paths many others miss. They naturally care about working hard but also about working smart. They wisely harness the power of *continual* learning to maximize their potential. All of these actions lead them ever closer to the success they desire. Are you one of them?

There has never been a more incredible time than now to create a better you and a more successful life. This is a meaningful opportunity to examine and evaluate what you want or don't want to keep doing. A time to reset your thinking and be clear regarding what matters to you and what does not. When you care about truly "getting" yourself and what makes you tick, you can hardly wait to put the magnificent power of your signature self-talk to work. How you *think* is how you will *live.* Therefore, it's more important than ever to dig in and design what you want to think about, believe, and work toward daily.

ACTIVATING FAITH-FUELED PLANS

Your signature self-talk is God's gift to you. It can produce growth, abundance, prosperity, and success when *directed* toward an excellent purpose. Imagine how life could be different when you fire yourself up on the inside and shape your own thinking. The endless possibilities are available to you anytime you step into your God-given influence and authority. Your signature self-talk can *speak life* into your own soul like nothing else can. It can activate your ability to think in bigger and better ways like nothing else ever will.

Start revving up your faith and preparing for more success. Believe in what God can do *in* you and *through* you so that you can be more, do more, and have more. He can not only resurrect old dreams, but He can also give you brand-new ones! There is no reason to limit Him with your unfocused thinking or your inability to receive it all. It is always possible to decide on changes you want to make and go to work designing the life you've dreamed of. Just like God did with me, He can use *you* to powerfully influence *you* and to get your faith-fueled plans into action!

Lastly, there is great importance in remembering that the purpose of God's call on your life is not just for your own benefit but for all of those whose lives you will play a role in transforming in the future. People are waiting for you to be in position; they are counting on you to keep passionately using your gifts and advancing in your mission. It's time to prepare for success, develop a winning belief system, upgrade your inner game, and step confidently into the ring with a solid offense strategy!

PREPARING FOR TRANSFORMATION

Now that we've laid the groundwork and become well prepared for transformation, we're finally ready to introduce the building blocks for creating your signature self-talk! With great anticipation, the next chapter will explain the key component, the sound of your voice. When you discover precisely how your own voice influences your mind and emotions, it will be clear why you will use your *signature sound* to speak your self-talk messages out loud.

Chapter 7

DISCOVERING YOUR SIGNATURE SOUND

"She can hear you, you know," the nurse whispered to me as she walked by and warmly touched my shoulder. She could see the lost look on my face as I sat quietly next to my mom's bed in the ICU. My beautiful eighty-six-year-old mom, my lifelong best friend, lay unconscious and on life support after a massive heart attack. I had talked to Mom just a few hours before it happened. If only I had known it would be the last time I would ever hear her voice and the last conversation we would ever have. It was still shocking to think how suddenly my entire world was turned upside down. Even more, how this could happen to such a strong, vibrant woman.

Filled with tubes and beeping machines monitoring every breath and heartbeat, Mom was unresponsive and fading fast. I knew these were the final moments I would ever spend with her. It just didn't seem real. I was painfully aware of every hour ticking by and how much every minute counted. Feeling numb and hopeless, I knew it was only a matter of time before she was gone, forever. I would have given anything for her to open her eyes, just one more time, so she could see that I was right there with her.

It could only have been the supernatural touch of God infusing me with the strength to endure the hours. Holding her hand, I kept waiting for some sign that Mom was still there. But nothing changed. I talked to her, prayed over her, sang quietly, and read scriptures to encourage her. Music was a big part of Mom's life, so I played her favorite music to comfort her, including a collection of recordings of her singing over the years.

Just as one of the playlists unexpectedly reached the end, a rare moment of stillness fell over the room. Suddenly, a sense of desperation washed over me as the reality of losing my mom began to sink in. Tears started to flow as I pulled my chair closer and leaned in toward her. My eyes closed tight; I rubbed her arm and silently tried to process the grief. Before I knew it, I was pouring out my heart. "You were always my first phone call, Mom. You have always been there for me." Words tumbled out in a crushing wave of emotion. "I just want to know that you're still here, Mom, and that somehow . . . you can hear me."

Finally, I opened my eyes and wiped my tears. I took a deep breath and slowly stood up. As I looked down at my mom's lifeless body, I bent over to kiss her forehead. At that very second, I noticed a tear rolling down her cheek. Then both cheeks! As I stared in shock and took in the miracle moment, time seemed to stand still. After hours of longing to connect somehow with Mom before our final good-bye, this was an incredible gift. We never got to share a word, and she never regained consciousness, but at that moment, I knew: she could hear me.

THE MIRACLE OF HEARING

After losing my mom, I thought a lot about the miracle of *hearing* in those last moments. It captured my heart and attention like never before. It spurred me on a mission to understand more about the gift of *sound* and how we are moved spiritually, mentally, emotionally, and physically by it. Each source I pursued confirmed our deep and powerful connection to sound, from Bible verses to scientific research and medical studies. The more digging I did, the more fascinating the idea of sound became to me.

From the beginning of life to our ending moments, our hearing plays a miraculous role. Remarkably, our ears are one of the first muscles formed in the womb, and our hearing is the last sense to go when passing from this earth. Without a doubt, we were created to be profoundly influenced by sound. Not only by incoming sounds but also by the sound we produce in our speech. Most importantly, God tells us that "faith comes from hearing" (Romans 10:17 NASB). What we *hear* can stir up our faith. Our spirit, mind, emotions, and body react uniquely to sound beyond anything I'd imagined.

As I continued to gain a broader understanding and appreciation for the gift of hearing, I was awestruck to discover that we hear the sound of our own voices in an extraordinary way. When we speak to ourselves *out loud*, we uniquely receive and process the information—not only in the way it resonates deeply in our hearts and minds, but it is also jam-packed with our feelings and emotions. I soon realized that it is our one-of-a-kind *sound* that gives our audible self-talk its very own *signature* quality.

The previous chapters discussed why our self-talk matters, what it affects, and its critical role in influencing and encouraging ourselves. But this chapter is the pivotal point to explain why signature self-talk is based upon speaking our messages *out loud*. The information that follows will make a compelling case for using the impressive influence of our *external* voice for our signature messages (backed up by scientific studies with supporting conclusions).

Before we move into the actual system for creating your signature self-talk in the next chapter, it's important to understand the multiple benefits of using your external voice to speak the messages you will design. It is the remarkable properties of your own individual sound that we will unpack in this chapter. Grab your coffee, and let's dive in to explore how your self-talk, delivered in your *signature sound*, can be the true game-changer!

THE HIDDEN KEY IN YOUR VOICE

It's easy to see that technology continues to move us toward a *voice-activated* world. Think of how your voice can already be used as a key. You can secure devices or unlock sensitive accounts. *Voice-controlled* products are everywhere, from vacuum cleaners and thermostats to computerized cars, TVs, and smartphones. It seems mind-boggling that you can *speak* a random question to a gadget in the palm of your hand and get an answer every time!

Using your voice as a key, you can access an infinite world of information anytime. Your voice can speak a command and get instant results on practically any conceivable topic. It can open up a world of endless choices to read, watch, or listen to. The point is your voice becomes the valuable key to setting it all in motion. As great as that may be, imagine using your voice daily to unlock, turn on, and command astonishing results in your *inner* world. Consider the vastly more profitable gateway you can enter—your own mind and heart—using your voice as a treasured key.

Just like you would give Google a clear verbal command to provide a specific result, you can speak clear commands to your mind to produce results. For instance, you can ask *yourself*, "What actions can I take today to be more motivated?" When you have a set purpose and expectation, you can simply put together well-defined wording to generate new ideas and lead yourself to practical solutions. Furthermore, your own voice becomes the priceless *key* to activating it all.

HOW SWEET THE SOUND

Do we take our ability to speak and freely express ourselves for granted? How often do we consider our effortless ability to *hear* ourselves and the world surrounding us each day? The fact that we can freely and naturally communicate is an incredible gift and a gratifying part of life.

Every part of us is wired for sound. Our day is filled with sound waves at vibrations and frequencies we never realize. Every time we use our voice, we are transmitting invisible sound waves. We are releasing energy and vibration unlike anyone else. *God* is moved by sound, *things* are driven by sound, and *we* are deeply affected by sound. Most exciting is that we have been given a sound exclusively our own. Like our fingerprint, every one of us has distinguishing features in our speaking *voice* that make us different. How is it unique? Our voice carries our individual style, traits, and expressions, making it our *signature* sound. All the more striking, we also have a particular way of talking to ourselves that is entirely our own. How we speak to ourselves is unlike the way any other person on this planet speaks to us.

Here is the vital connection I want you to catch. Your voice has tremendous influence built into it. It influences *you* as it carries your thoughts, feelings, emotions, and energy. But what can supercharge the impact is combining your signature *voice* with your personal signature *messages to yourself.* When you use these two powerful forces together, it becomes your very own *signature self-talk*. Delivering your self-talk *out loud*, in your own voice, boosts the level of influence. Your individual sound custom-frames every word you speak and every message you convey. It affects every single word you form. As you create *specific* ideas into messages, they become your blueprints for improving any area of your life. Your unique voice can significantly activate every signature message you craft to upgrade your life.

With one-of-a-kind access to your mind, your voice is incomparable. High or low, loud or soft, it's woven into your being and a part of who you are. It carries extraordinary power, authority, and, most of all, believability. Like no other sound, your brain and mind's *receptivity* to your voice is unmatched in its ability to comprehend the meaning and emotion in every word you speak.

As you grasp all these hidden elements, you will realize the phenomenal impact your signature qualities can have on your life. With this in mind, consider your self-talk as the signature *code* that can be used to program the direction of everywhere you want to go. Once you begin skillfully learning how to design your signature self-talk in the next chapter, it will give you the potential to change your world, inside and out.

YOUR UNIQUE VOICE
There is an array of emotions embedded in your voice far beyond the words you speak. Your speech is packed with personality, feelings, and a range of expressions, from laughter to heartache. Along with being able to communicate love, excitement, pain, and fear, your voice carries the ability to heal, encourage, motivate, and empathize. With all of these hallmarks, your voice is a powerful tool for transformation.

How does your personal sound capture your *own* attention? It carries authority, establishes identity, and conveys much more than information. Therefore, speaking new, purpose-driven thoughts with passion can crack old codes and break through previous cycles of thinking. Imagine using your signature sound to its full potential to eliminate broken, destructive, upsetting thinking patterns. What if you used it to uplift, strengthen, motivate, and encourage yourself? In short, the personalization of your self-talk, delivered in your own voice, can stir you at the deepest levels.

When we use the dynamic influence of our signature self-talk to speak into our own lives, we can discover a side of ourselves that we've only dreamed of. I've seen talented musicians grow into extraordinary performers after being too afraid to sing in front of anyone. I've witnessed entrepreneurs who became polished business professionals after they had been too fearful even to share an idea. It has been inspiring to see salespeople develop into top-selling agents after they had once been too nervous to close a deal. Even more, I've seen individuals proud to walk in their own personal style of self-expression when they once didn't dare to be different in any way. In every transformation, the individual's signature voice played a distinct role in developing the courage to take their place in the world.

Your voice can literally become a life-altering instrument of change in your own life. It can influence and shape how you feel about yourself. What you speak out loud to yourself, in your signature sound, can heighten your awareness, increase your clarity, and change your state. Like a beam of light hitting the darkness, it can bring what you are processing inside to the outside. Still more remarkable, your voice can help to unlock and rev up your best qualities and highest performance. Consider how developing specific purpose-driven self-talk can expand your skills, increase productivity, or reinforce valuable habits and best practices. As you continually speak out the behaviors and qualities you desire, you begin thinking, acting, and expecting to become that person. The best of the best of you will come shining through! These fantastic features are all wrapped up in the incredible gift of your own signature sound.

Throughout your life, you must have a safe and trustworthy voice you can always count on. That voice is yours. Genuine, raw, and strikingly transparent, with no hidden agendas. What other sound could ever compare? Grounded in trusting God and based on your core values, you can create your *own* dynamic messages to meditate on, uplift you, or power you up at any time. You have nothing to hide, and you can trust that you are secure and acting in your best interest. Your voice is not just for the world *outside;* it is vital to your world *inside* as you dare to deeply know, like, and trust yourself like never before.

HOW YOUR BRAIN REACTS TO YOUR VOICE

While *visual* stimulation always gets attention, I believe the miraculous power and *influence* of your *vocal sound* are not discussed enough. As we can see, it has a dynamic all of its own. Your brain tunes into more than just your words. Consciously and unconsciously, it picks up on your emotions, expressions, meanings, and all the hidden nuances in between. It listens for the voice *within* your voice. It's more than sound because it's *your* sound. It's intimate, trusted, and significant. Ironically, you hear it outside as you *feel* it inside. Consider how the ultimate familiarity of your voice penetrates your mind. Never underestimate what your beautiful, God-given, one-of-a-kind sound can accomplish. Of every voice in the world, *yours* is different, and your mind and brain know and embrace it.

When you talk, you hear yourself both externally and internally. It's a sound you recognize and understand more than any other speech. It really doesn't matter if you don't like hearing your own voice. When you press past judging it, you realize that your signature sound can speak more intensely into your heart, mind, spirit, and soul than anyone else could. Your brain is highly activated by and influenced by your own unique voice. Your signature style, tempo, timbre, and tone are distinctive and known. Once you learn to use your voice *proactively* to influence your own mind, what can be accomplished is staggering.

I have discovered that our brain seems to wake up knowing our voice will convey an important message. Our mind comes to attention when it hears what has been exclusively designed not only *by* us but *for* us. It's a different experience when we speak directly into our own intimate areas of pain, weakness, hopes, or dreams. Our self-talk, speaking to ourselves out loud, resonates when we speak up *to* ourselves and *for* ourselves, especially in the delicate parts of our life. It could never be spoken more perfectly than by our signature voice. Consider all the possibilities when we get our self-talk in motion in our own *influential* sound. We can turn it into a motivation machine, a wellness-producing powerhouse, and our most significant asset.

WHAT YOUR VOICE COMMUNICATES

So, what does science tell us? I promised to keep things simple, so I will only touch on two fascinating studies to support my findings. But overall, the research is consistent that the amount of information our voice can communicate is astounding! Let's start with a 2017 study in the journal *American Psychologist* titled "Voice-Only Communication Enhances Empathic Accuracy."[12] Through five experiments, a comparison was made using the *voice*, the *face*, and *nonverbal* expressions. The purpose was to find out which one proved best for *accurately* judging the emotions and feelings of *other* people while they were interacting. The result? Remarkably, *voice-only communication* was the *most precise* channel to express and communicate emotion between people. It even surpassed facial expressions! This outcome highlighted that the voice *alone* allows us to pick up on vocal cues in *what* is said and *how* it is said.

How does this tie into using our voice in our signature self-talk? Consider that if our voice accurately conveys our internal state to *others*, how much more can it profoundly communicate with *us*? Track with me as we zoom in closer with one more revealing study demonstrating how remarkably our voice can affect us.

The authoritative journal *Proceedings of the National Academy of Sciences (PNAS)* published results in January 2016 from a study on the influence of our voice.[13] To break it down in simple terms, a team conducted research that involved *secretly* altering a participant's emotional tone in their recorded voice. They changed the pitch to make the person sound either happy, sad, or fearful. Then they observed the individual's reactions as they listened to their own recorded voice.

Interestingly, the researchers found that the participants rarely detected the adjustments. But most shocking was that the individuals aligned their *current* emotional state with the emotion they heard on the recording! This outcome suggests that the emotions carried in our voice can highly influence our overall emotional state. The leader of the research study, Jean-Julien Aucouturier, summed it up by stating, "It is really a striking result that participants ended up updating their emotional state in response to whether their own voices were made to sound happy, sad, or anxious."[14] So what does all of this mean? The main point I want you to catch in these findings is that our voices can powerfully influence and *alter* our moods and emotions. Let me show you how we can leverage this to full advantage in our signature self-talk.

REVERSE ENGINEERING INFLUENCE

Keeping in mind all we've learned regarding the absolute magnitude of influence in our signature voice, I want to introduce my own theory based on my experience. I've found that we can *reverse engineer* how we influence *ourselves*. We can use the brilliant capabilities in our signature voice to intentionally influence our minds. Essentially, we can be strategic in altering our *own moods and state* to produce positive results. How? By creating and using *pre-designed* signature messages with *desirable* emotions that *we* build into them. In other words, instead of our feelings dictating to us, we control and *implant* the emotions we want to lead the way. We design, speak, and record positive, motivating, faith-driven, hopeful, and empowering messages to listen to and influence ourselves. Then our mega persuasive recorded voice goes to work to help us alter and improve our emotions and state of mind as we listen. Not only will our brain believe what we are telling it consistently, but it will also be convinced by our influential voice relaying the message.

How can we use this strategy to pull the highest level of influence out of our voice? To demonstrate, let's make a simple comparison to check out how different our listening levels can be and what they can mean. First, how often do you really hear or pay attention to your voice in action every day? It can seem pretty automatic to merely speak whenever you want to express yourself, right? Typically, you are not focused on or tuned into *how* you are affected by your voice or what you say. Speaking freely and hearing your voice is just a regular part of your everyday routine, and you move on. Let's call this Level 1 Listening.

Now, let's change the dynamics a bit. What if you recorded your voice reading something general and played it back to listen? Somehow you would become more tuned in to judging how your voice sounds, your emotional tone, and the quality of your speech. Your brain appears to pay more attention to what you say and how you say it. Consciously and unconsciously, you mysteriously pick up on new things you did not hear or even notice in your voice during everyday live conversation. Consider this Level 2 Listening.

Lastly, what if you recorded your voice with a specific message to yourself that had deep personal meaning? You spoke it with unmistakable passion, intent, and emotion. Imagine your voice energetically bringing your thoughts to life as it describes the details of your most exciting goal or dream. Somehow, in this version, you notice and care more about what you say, how you say it, and the feelings and emotions attached. You "get" and deeply resonate with what you hear. This, my friend, is the unequaled power and influence of your signature self-talk at work. This is what I call Level 3 Listening. More than just hearing, you *feel* what you are hearing at the deepest levels. Only you can catch all the little sparks on that recording that will keep igniting you. The more you listen, the more impact it can make.

LEAVING "ME" A MESSAGE

In my own life, recording myself speaking to myself has proven to be the most revolutionary aspect of my signature self-talk. It *captures* the combined influence of my signature *sound*, personal *message*, and heartfelt *emotions*. Best of all, now in a *reusable* form, the impact is maximized. How? Because it is easy to keep listening by simply replaying the recording. I can continue to implant the information deeper as I repeatedly feed my mind the *same* phenomenal message. Listening to the message over and over keeps the message at the forefront of my thoughts, empowering me and driving me closer to my goal every day.

Like a catchy song, when you keep influencing yourself with your recorded signature messages, you begin to hear them in your head, even when they're not playing. The more you listen, the more they become ingrained in your thinking. Whether they are your personal power prayers, declarations, gratitude list, pep talk, or goal blueprints, they get planted in your mind and memory as you repeat the same messages. As they really sink into your mind, spirit, and soul, you begin to know them "by heart." You can even reach the point where you can chime in with your own recorded voice to ramp up an even more significant effect.

BUILDING A SELF-TALK ARSENAL

Your *recorded signature messages* are your ammunition, reinforcement, and personal life solutions that are locked, loaded, and ready to go! You are strengthening your mind and moxie whenever you listen. These messages will consistently build you up and keep you on track, especially when you need it the most. After all, it is you who has personally designed and approved each one of your self-talk messages. It's invigorating to form and maintain a powerful arsenal of godly thoughts to draw from each day. At the simple push of a button, you can keep them playing loudly in your heart and mind to *influence* your thinking, update your emotions, and *alter* your state. Suppose life throws you a curveball and you start sliding toward negativity. You can use your recorded messages to interrupt that pattern and head your thoughts and *emotions* in a better direction. Before you know it, your ingrained messages will begin to surface and cut off what had been running before.

Imagine having your soul-stirring messages at your fingertips in your most vulnerable moments. If you wake up feeling directionless one day, grab your passionate recording describing your clear vision of where you plan to go, what you plan to do, and how amazing it will feel. You don't want to search haphazardly for something to fill your mind when stressed and overwhelmed. It's too easy to head straight into the danger zone of discouragement. Reach directly for your arsenal instead!

When you use the synergy of your own messaging and highly influential voice in a repeatable audio recording, your heartfelt desire, energy, and emotion can continue to drive you. Instead of drifting, you will stay engaged. Moreover, you will move toward what you keep focusing on and thinking about. All you have to do is one simple thing every day. Just push PLAY!

Let's keep up the momentum and start putting all the pieces together! In the next chapter, we will expand on the idea of using the influence in your *recorded* voice as we move into the four simple steps for building your high-performance signature self-talk system.

Chapter 8

CREATING YOUR SIGNATURE SYSTEM

On a majestic mountain slope in Colorado lie the ruins of a gigantic tree. During this forest giant's long life, it withstood countless avalanches and storms spanning over four centuries. If examined closely, it is clear the tree was also struck by lightning at least fourteen times. It seemed as if nothing could conquer this formidable tree. That is, until the day an army of tiny little beetles attacked it. These insignificant little insects began eating their way through the bark, destroying the *inner strength* of the tree and eventually leveling it to the ground. At last, the battling mammoth of the woods succumbed to beetles so small you could crush them between your thumb and forefinger.

Humans, like trees, are endowed with similar characteristics. Somehow, we manage to muster the strength to overcome the storms, the avalanches, and the lightning blasts of life, only to have our hearts eaten out by little "beetles" of *worry* and *stress*. Instead of coming against the day-to-day harmful thoughts in our lives, we sometimes go out of our way to collect them. The "beetles" that destroy *our* inner core come from financial trouble, family problems, illness, lack of love, bitterness, jealousy, anger, depression, and so much more. The distress of being unhappy with ourselves, believing that others have let us down, or sometimes feeling as if no one really cares can systematically eat away at us on the *inside*. In all these things, we must understand how to properly shield and protect ourselves from the little beetles that can work against us on the inside. We need a strategy to stop what can persistently erode our thoughts and slowly try to take us down.

Let's be honest: as simple as it may sound to think positively, control our thoughts, and stay focused on our goals, we know it will *always* be an ongoing challenge. It's a lifelong battle that requires us to stay on our toes and be well equipped to *keep* our thinking in a strong, healthy condition. We need a reliable system to help us manage our thoughts and, just as importantly, to energize our faith and ignite the power we need every day.

God has made us directly responsible for managing ourselves, including our own thought lives. We can take that responsibility seriously or leave our thinking to random chance. When we know how to use our God-given authority to routinely speak into our lives and circumstances, we can actively do our part to live our best lives every day.

LIVING YOUR BEST LIFE

God gives us the power to shape *ourselves* and our lives, although most people never learn how to take full advantage of it. For instance, we can shape our food choices and nutrition intake, sleep, exercise, and personal growth, to name just a few. Our inner self-control is available anytime to awaken us to *do* more and strengthen us to *become* more. When our minds are renewed, it creates awareness and discovery and can spark our desire to reach for change. As we learn to tap into the strength and power of God in us, we will find that we have *everything* we need to begin *any* transformation.

This chapter will give you the framework to build your signature self-talk system. It is the number one strategy I have used extensively and successfully in my life, career, and business for many years. It has been the key to improving how I talk to, influence, and encourage myself daily. This method has not only proven to be the tipping point to empower me in the worst of times, but it has also helped me gain ground fast in reaching goals. Most of all, it has helped me stand firm against the little beetles that can be the silent killers in my everyday life. It can be of remarkable value once you understand how it works.

This little *system* has been an answer to prayer. God has used it to touch my life and strengthen me from the inside out. It has provided clarity when I couldn't think straight, invigorated hope when overwhelmed, and instilled peace of mind in uncomfortable storms. It has helped me uncover my most profound creativity and solve life problems. I've used it to help me master my thoughts and emotions and to acquire new skills faster, more easily, and more proficiently. I could speak volumes about how my simple system has become my most incredible self-talk tool to boost my mood and regain self-control and direction. I consider it miraculous, yet it is so easy that anyone can do it.

It was essential to lay the groundwork in previous chapters in order to prepare the way for unrolling this technique. Why? Without fully understanding and appreciating how you can influence and encourage yourself and the significance of using your vocal influence to speak your signature messages, this system would not hold the same weight. But now you have the building blocks necessary to connect all the pieces and run with the new concept being unpacked in this chapter.

THE 4-STEP DARE SYSTEM

Let me start by laying out the basics of what I refer to as my 4-Step DARE System, an *action plan* for creating and plugging signature self-talk messages into our daily thinking. DARE stands for Design, Activate, Repeat, and Elevate. Simple, right?

Before I break down each step, let's do a quick overview. Consider each signature self-talk message you create as a dare you give yourself. You are daring to influence and encourage yourself and to fire up the necessary faith, strength, power, and courage in yourself to think or do something in your life.

Step 1: **D**ESIGN. You design a signature self-talk message specific to your needs, goals, or desires.

Step 2: **A**CTIVATE. You speak and activate your message in an audio recording.

Step 3: **R**EPEAT. You put the power of repetition to work as you keep listening to your recorded message to influence your mind, shape your thinking, and improve your life.

Step 4: **ELEVATE**. You officially acknowledge and celebrate how your life has been upgraded.

Every time you use this easy system, you will be daring yourself to ignite and use the resources God has given you. Your signature self-talk becomes a golden asset to build more excellence in your life. When the DARE System is implemented, it fires you up *internally*. It puts your faith into action by producing specific self-talk to bridge the gap between where you are now and where you want to go. Since your mind will reap what you plant, it's important to get busy planting worthwhile things that can start growing and moving you in the right direction immediately.

Now, let's take a closer look at how you can use the DARE System to talk to, influence, and encourage yourself daily. Once again, you have nothing to lose and everything to gain!

TALK TO, INFLUENCE, AND ENCOURAGE YOURSELF

The goal is for you to learn the 4-Step DARE process, run with it, and *enjoy* using it. It is a technique to help you *thrive* on the inside, no matter what life may bring. It is meant to keep you in a position of strength as you *dare* to initiate action and keep advancing in life. Best of all, it challenges the one major downfall that ensnares most people: *inconsistency*. The 4-Step DARE System takes you far beyond short-lived solutions that burn out quickly. Instead, it gives you a form of *ongoing influence and encouragement* that will carry you the distance. It can be life altering when you master this ability.

Think of the DARE System as a blank canvas to start designing your *internal support system*. It is the literal application of God's Word in your life. You have complete control of putting your signature qualities to work to infuse your mind, spirit, and soul. The process becomes quicker and easier every time you use the DARE System. You gain momentum when you move into action and use your signature self-talk. As your repertoire grows, you will master the development of your self-talk messages to tackle anything you want to boost or improve in your life. It's time to believe in your God-given ability to inspire *yourself*.

God has not only given you a sound mind but the absolute ability to use it in full force. Your signature self-talk will put all of that to work in new and phenomenal ways. You are fully equipped, but only you can activate your signature self-talk. When you do, you will realize your capacity to accelerate your own progress. Rather than leaving your thoughts scattered, this system will help you organize your ideas to produce a better way of thinking, believing, and living every day. A trusted system makes all the difference in leading you to the results you want to achieve in your life, leadership, career, or business. Now, let's break down each of the four steps in the DARE System with more clarity and detail.

STEP 1: DESIGN
The first step in the DARE process is to *design* your signature self-talk message. It is exciting to know that you

can construct your own soul-stirring messages that can transform *any* area of your life. With practice, you will become an expert at crafting your *signature messages* to drive results and build an impressive self-talk *arsenal*. After all, how can you have a vigorous faith *walk* without compelling faith *talk*, right?

Start by identifying a specific area in your life you want to target. What's on your mind that you want to do, change, or become? What do you feel led to strengthen, clarify, or build in new ways? What blueprints are you ready to lay out for a new idea, goal, or vision you want to bring to life? Do you want to deeply embed specific prayers or scriptures in your heart to encourage yourself and stay on fire for God? You can customize and personalize your messages exactly how you want them. Little by little, you will establish a private collection that will be distinctly focused on what you want to put in your mind and what you want to happen in your life. Your signature messages are meant for your eyes and ears only. They will help sustain, recharge, and build you up in your personal life behind closed doors.

The real clout of every signature self-talk message comes from using your own unique ideas, expressions, and style. You command every aspect, so make it individual, private, and deeply meaningful to *you*. When you focus on topics that have a specific purpose for you, they will resonate more and more as you continually plant them in your heart and mind. Your message can be long or short, intense or relaxed, and focused on any topic. (We will learn more about specific styles in the next chapter.) You can plug your message anywhere in your routine or daily activities, from quiet listening to playing your audio recording while driving, exercising, or brushing your teeth. The convenience and portable nature of audio is excellent. You decide on your own campaign of when, where, and how often you want to absorb your specific message for the results you're hoping for. You can also change or update any part of your signature pieces anytime.

Like an arrow, you want the messages you shoot into your mind to hit the right target. How you line up your specific words and intentions can make or break the final result. Be clear about what you want to *say* and what you *mean*. Speak directly to the issue, vision, or goal. State distinctly what you *want*, not what you *don't want*. The detail you use will affect how your mind hears, uses, and responds to the input. Your brain needs precise information to move you toward the right outcome. Trust your gut in making your message positive and passionate. You instinctively know what words, tones, and thoughts will light you up. Try to become more self-aware to understand how you're naturally wired. Look for emotionally charged words familiar to you that will trigger your mind in all the right ways.

For example, you could create a specific message to form a new habit of getting up one hour earlier to start your day with an energizing *hour of power*. To fortify your mind, body, and spirit, you focus on three specific activities: exercise, prayer, and reading. Get a clear sense of how it will look and feel to take charge of this hour to kick off your day purposefully and catapult your confidence. Begin by constructing the image of yourself moving into action as the alarm goes off and enthusiastically outline what you will do, *why* you're doing it, and your determination to do it! Do you have specific workout clothes prepared? Is your favorite water bottle filled and ready to go? What exercise do you have planned to get your blood pumping? Picture yourself smiling and in motion, declaring, "I can do this!" Next, narrate the scene of settling into your favorite spot to sit quietly and sip a hot cup of coffee as you pray, read, and reflect in preparation for the day ahead. As you clearly describe how you look and feel in each segment of your well-organized plan, the right target is being set in your thoughts. Ultimately, the mission of your signature message is to persuade your mind of all the unique and irresistible benefits of the new habit or activity. Details matter! The more you give your brain to work with, the clearer and more appealing the image it can move toward.

Lastly, always use present tense wording in stating your messages. God gives us a clear example with this command: "Let the weak say, I *am* strong" (Joel 3:10 NKJV, italics mine). Declaring the outcome as if it has already been achieved is fundamental. For example, I am, I have, I make, I do, I earn, I weigh. Paint a vivid picture with your words, voice, and emotions that can help you see and feel your vision as if it is *already* true.

ADDING PERSONAL PERSUASION: We all have something, some job or task, that feels like a continuous struggle to make ourselves do. We want to get it done but don't *feel* like doing it. For whatever reason, we find ourselves avoiding and putting it off. Imagine if we could alter our thinking and get it done more quickly. The DARE System gives us a highly effective method to overcome this obstacle of procrastination or avoidance. But even more, as we design our custom messages, one little technique can build in an extra layer of personal persuasion. We can *purposely* attach extreme *pleasure* to a task, activity, or goal to sway our own thinking and level of enthusiasm. Shifting our minds to believe something is pleasurable rather than unpleasant can change how we act and feel toward it.

The trick is to persuade our minds that we *desire* to do it. How? We design a signature message and fire up a campaign to tie massive pleasure to the specific task or goal we want to accomplish. Once again, it is a matter of putting our signature message to work to influence our thinking. We provide our minds with *new* feelings and beliefs about the project we want to get done or the habit we would like to command. Remember, our mind actively believes what we tell it. Our intensely uplifting message can describe how much we love the task or activity, how great it makes us feel, and how it fills us with pleasure! As our voice outlines all the tremendous benefits, we make it clear to our minds that we are thrilled about doing it.

As we purposely dominate our thinking with our *pleasure version,* we frame our task or goal as irresistible and appealing. Before long, our mind views the task as fun and desirable. As a result, we find ourselves drawn toward it rather than away from it.

STEP 2: ACTIVATE
The next step in the DARE System is to *activate* your signature message by making it an *audio recording*. When you record your signature message, you freeze it in time and transform it into a *repeatable* form. This is the actual game changer. When you now have your

signature message *on demand,* you can actively feed it to your mind at the push of a button. Listening to your voice consistently deliver the *same* life-altering message to your mind is intensely persuasive. Each time you hear it, it will inspire your thinking, sharpen your mind, shape your life, and, most importantly, build your faith. Remember, faith comes by *hearing (Romans 10:17)*! When we realize how *everything* we hear can affect our faith, we recognize how critical it is to ramp up the self-talk messages that will strengthen and build our faith daily.

As discussed in chapter 7, your heart's desires can come wondrously alive in your signature messages. Your brain resonates with your unique sound, energy, emotion, and sentiment that shine through in your spoken words. Like when one of your all-time favorite songs begins to play, your attention is sparked, and your mind and body respond. You are moved as you hear your signature sound, style, and feelings tightly woven into every word you say.

MAKING YOUR AUDIO RECORDING: As you read or speak your message to make your digital audio recording, ensure your energy and mood are high. How you *deliver* the signature message is imperative. You set the vibe. The key is to fully engage in everything you are stating, expressing, and believing *as* you record your message. Ultimately, what you implant *now* will grow your arsenal to better equip your mind ahead.

Pick a time when you are fresh, focused, and enthusiastic. You want the best of you to be captured and relayed. Maximize your influence by speaking your message with confidence and authority. Don't be afraid to be firm or indicate excitement. Appeal to your own emotions and communicate clearly with genuine conviction. Just as important, make sure your delivery is smooth and spoken clearly. When you activate your message, your brain will pick up and process *everything* it hears from you.

Your signature messages certainly don't have to be perfect; they merely have to originate from the authentic you. There is no pressure. You can change or redo any message to produce a version you feel comfortable with. You are worth the investment. While no one else is listening, you can be assured that every part of *you* is tuned in to what is being communicated! Your signature pieces will become your private collection and a valuable asset to play again and again to shape and enrich your life.

> **"Be careful how you think; your life is shaped by your thoughts."**
> **—Proverbs 4:23 GNT**

Whether recording your personal prayers, signature affirmations, a pep talk, or a blueprint of your goals and dreams for the future, delivering your message to your mind in your own recorded voice is unlike any other influence. Far beyond just *setting* intentions, you will be boldly *speaking* and *declaring* them. Don't just talk about your goals; talk about your unshakable faith in achieving them. Describe all the benefits you will receive. Instead of just expressing what you are excited about becoming, talk about your deep conviction to become that better version of yourself. Speak with confidence and certainty. Allow your faith to be built up. Realize what your faith coming through your voice can do! God tells us clearly and directly that He acknowledges and responds to our faith: "Because of your faith, it will happen" (Matthew 9:29 NLT).

Your recorded messages will uplift and help you in every area of your life. When you need to remain steady under pressure in dark times, disruption, or adversity, you will know how to rouse God's gifts inside you to stand firm. Why? Simply because you have already spoken about it, heard it, and done it so many times before!

This simple step to secure your best thoughts in a power-packed audio message will supercharge how your brain perceives and remembers the seeds of encouragement you have planted to create an extraordinary life. Use your imagination to picture your cells lighting up all over your body, and celebrate the healthy, positive thoughts you are feeding your mind daily with your signature self-talk messages.

> **"Whatever we plant in our subconscious mind and nourish with repetition and emotion will one day become a reality."**
> **—Earl Nightingale**

STEP 3: REPETITION

Step three in the DARE System involves putting the dynamic power of *repetition* to work in order to deeply embed your message. Once you've invested the effort to record your signature message, it's time to begin *saturating* your mind with it. Hearing and experiencing your voice convey life-altering thoughts is unlike any other sound. No longer will valuable and uplifting information be fleeting when you strategically keep it *repeating!*

Imagine the ease of having your signature recording conveniently ready for you to hit play at any time on your smartphone or other devices. Because it is preset and ready to go, you have eliminated the common barrier that keeps so many people from following through; a complicated or time-consuming process that can deter you from taking action. As you continue to soak in your signature messages, you continually reinforce what you have decided you want your reality to be. Build faith in what you're hearing, and let what you're hearing build your faith. The single decision to listen *repetitively* to your recording can lead the way to every turning point you desire. Your voice will supply the right thoughts to focus on and remind you *daily* of what you are working toward and how excited you are to make it happen.

INFLUENCING PERSISTENTLY: As you can see, once your signature message is saved in a form that can repeatedly influence you, it is just a matter of persistently applying that influence. Your job is to keep listening and allow your recorded self-talk to update your state of mind and motivate you. It becomes a brilliant reinforcement strategy as you consistently pay attention to what you've determined you want to achieve or change in your life. It is the ultimate daily reminder to spark your memory and take your self-talk to new levels. Repetition is persuasive. As you activate your influence, it will keep moving you in the right direction, both inside and out. You can knock down resistance and trigger change when you stay proactive in feeding your mind with your transformational messages.

CREATING YOUR SIGNATURE SYSTEM

As you continue listening to your recorded messages, you use your voice to help you move through obstacles, focus on solutions, and boldly run toward your giants. Everything you jump-start *inside* will soon become a reflex and a habit to position you better in life *outside*. You are proactively strengthening and conditioning yourself. Best of all, you will remain faithful in using what God put inside you. You are doing your part to fortify your inner resources and grow more equipped to face new situations.

The 4-Step DARE System gives you a solid plan to help you keep growing and advancing. Best of all, it is entirely under your control. Are you willing to separate from the crowd? Will you choose to step beyond what others do? While others around you may struggle to clarify or write down their goals, you can find great satisfaction in knowing you're skillfully surpassing the norm. Even more, you are becoming your own efficiency expert using the DARE System. As you stay activated inside, you will live with more clarity and intentionality. Setting yourself up to win and succeed at the highest levels leads to the final step in the DARE System.

STEP 4: ELEVATE
Step four completes the DARE cycle. It's all about *officially* celebrating the *elevation* you experience when you've upgraded your life and accomplished what you *dared to do*. The outside change may be rewarding, but even more, your *internal process* and self-talk journey is the actual crowning achievement. You formulated the plan, outlined the road map, and summoned the courage to reach your destination. In faith, you pressed in,

influenced and encouraged yourself, and transformed your life. You are no longer *who* you were and no longer *where* you were. It's important to realize how far you've come and the more resistant foundation you've built. Remember, success breeds success!

CELEBRATING YOUR WINS: Every win must be celebrated in order to invigorate your attitude, confidence level, and skills. Stop to think about the new ground you've taken, how you've pushed beyond old boundary lines, and rejoice in how you have enlarged your vision. In fact, every improvement you make in your *personal* life will also help you soar in your *professional* journey. Every victory contributes to more success in every area of your life. Make it memorable and mark it well! Most importantly, don't forget to deposit your new achievement into your courage account and add it to your gratitude list of all God has done in your life. Elevate proudly, making sure you take the culminating last step of celebrating your self-talk successes!

FAST-TRACKING RESULTS
There is a common thread in achieving goals for all of us. We want to reach them faster! Study after study has shown that you can significantly increase your chances of achieving your goals simply by writing them down. Furthermore, repetition has been cheered as the key to memory formation and mastery. Imagine being able to improve your success rate by combining your signature self-talk's influence with these powerhouse elements—writing your goals down and repeatedly listening to them in a recorded message to yourself. Using these principles *together*—the written form, your influential voice, and

repetition—can be a significant breakthrough for those serious about personal and professional development. It's a win-win-win! The DARE System will keep your goals firmly in front of you and your mind actively working to achieve them. What you focus on, you move toward. The more you listen to your goal-oriented audio messages, the more impact they will have in helping you advance closer and closer to your target. You structure each campaign and decide how to dial the repetitions up or down. It's entirely up to you and your level of motivation.

The more you use the DARE System to reinforce how you want your life to prosper, the more you can fast-track results and nail your accomplishments. You will keep building momentum when you are relentless about giving your mind clear direction. Think of the strides you will make as you stay consistent in providing your mind with a clear voice and message. Some messages will be for a reason, others for a season, and a few for a lifetime. Go after opportunities wholeheartedly, and make every day and every message count!

STAYING CONSISTENT IN YOUR MISSION
With the DARE System, some people may experience breakthroughs quickly, and for others, breakthroughs may take longer. The point is to stay consistent in your mission. Keep listening to your signature messages. Keep exercising your faith and building your thought muscles as you press toward the results you want to achieve. Realize that you are on a valuable journey to slowly chip away at old thinking and form *new* patterns. Day by day, the more you listen to your faith-fueled messages, the

more they will shape your mind and strengthen your *internal support system.*

Ultimately, you alone control what role you will play in making any area of your life shift from struggling to flourishing. God designed *you* to be the one to stir up your own gifts inside, not to rely on other people, places, or things to stir them up for you. Why would He continue to pour great blessings into you if you never use what He deposits in you? How can He bless your efforts if there are no efforts to bless? Only you can activate the inner gifts that can move you to new levels of abundance and prosperity. The principle is that you will be given more when you are faithful with less. Likewise, every little good decision can soon lead to enormous payoffs.

As you can see, it is much more than simply feeding your mind messages; it's the signature way you create and implant them that supercharges the impact. When you invest the time into developing the signature self-talk that will serve you and strengthen you at the deepest levels, watch your success multiply in every area of your thinking and your life. You are close to a breakthrough in all your heart's desires that God has waiting for you. I dare you to be brave enough to do the work, capture your golden messages, and use them consistently in order to keep elevating and celebrating your life.

In the next chapter, we will check out specific messages styles, recording and listening options, and other practical ideas for setting up a daily routine for your signature self-talk.

Chapter 9

OPTIONS, ROUTINES, AND APPLICATIONS

Like a spirited symphony, every signature self-talk piece you compose becomes music to your ears. It shifts the atmosphere in your heart and triggers the vibrations in your soul. Sometimes it's a soft touch to calm you down. Other times it can rise to a dynamic pitch to ignite everything in you! The distinct harmony of your voice with your mind and body can be mesmerizing. Best of all, you are the conductor who hears every intricate detail and orchestrates the entire experience. Major or minor, the notes strike a powerful chord and flow into the cascade of sound to influence the beautiful masterpiece that is your *thought life*.

> "Pay close attention to what you hear.
> The closer you listen,
> the more understanding you will be given—and
> you will receive even more."
> —Mark 4:24 NLT

Whatever mission, vision, or challenge you face, be assured that you can design a brilliant signature message to speak to it. This chapter will provide practical ideas to help you organize and set up your self-talk routine. As you gear up to start operating in your signature gifts and using the 4-Step DARE System, you will have some options to help you launch into designing and using your self-talk confidently.

PRIMING YOURSELF

Think of your signature self-talk as a means of *priming* yourself for what's ahead in your life. Like priming a pump, your signature message can stimulate and prepare you for action. In other words, your self-talk can encourage you internally *before* you venture out externally. You get mentally prepared *first*. As you influence your own *desire for change or growth*, your signature self-talk can make you *hungry* to start!

For instance, imagine listening intently to your signature recording a week before you want to start a new healthy eating plan. Before you even begin the program, your recorded message lays out the exciting results ahead by forming a clear picture of all the upcoming benefits and good feelings. As you keep priming your mind, you are influencing yourself to know what you will do, how amazing it will be, and how great you will feel. As you build the anticipation in advance, you kick-start your momentum and prepare yourself to take action. What you have been telling your mind is not only getting you pumped and excited but also conditioning your mind to look forward to what's coming. Do you see how effectively your self-talk can influence your mind *before* you officially begin?

OPTIONS FOR COMPOSING SELF-TALK MESSAGES

Let's jump in by looking at four basic design options for forming your signature messages. You can choose a *structured style,* a *free-flow style,* an *interactive style,* or a *study and learning* technique.

Style 1: Structured (Written). In this format, you will write out your complete signature message *in advance* in order to read and record it later. The structured style is excellent when you want to organize your thoughts or information in a specific way. This format can be highly beneficial when you want to formulate a plan or a blueprint to follow closely. Whether it's habits or behaviors you desire to change, or goals you want to accomplish, laying out the details can create clear-cut intention and motivation.

Your signature message can be based strictly on your original ideas and content, other materials, or a mixture of both. Either way, the point is to personally compile, arrange, and shape the information to make it your own. Your exclusive arrangement and special touches mold it into your own unique *signature* message.

You can pull inspiration from various quality sources, including scriptures, books, quotes, magazines, poems, song lyrics, articles, training courses, sermons, or motivational material, to name a few. The key is to carefully select, approve, and make all the content hyper-personal and relevant to you and your situation. Whatever content you choose, the value in this style is that your message will end up in two different forms, both written and recorded. You can use them separately or together. For maximum benefit, you can combine looking at the written words of your message with listening. This practice can make a more profound impression on your mind for even deeper penetration and faster results.

Style 2: Free-Flow. I refer to this incredible message style as free-flow. It comes from whatever flows naturally from you as you speak to record your message. It's spontaneous, conversational, and descriptive. It can be long or short, calming or intense. It focuses on stirring up your emotions and connecting with how you want to see yourself and feel. Once again, you would speak as if you have already conquered the feat you are aiming for and are experiencing how fantastic it is. There should be a distinct tone of enthusiasm to tell your mind clearly and firmly that this is what you *want* to do and how much you *love* doing it. It's best to focus on only one issue or topic if you use this style. Whether determining to stay calm while driving in heavy traffic, confidently lead an important event, or tackle a major project ahead of you, the free-flow recording technique requires you to create a convincing argument of the massive pleasure involved in the outcome you're focusing on. Thoughtfully describe, in detail, how the end result will light you up in every imaginable way!

You can also use free-flow messages to create a short, intense burst of encouragement to empower you. This is beneficial to address a pressing issue weighing heavily on your mind or even a goal you want to pursue with full force. Your message should be passionate and emotionally charged in a spirit of strength and overcoming. Entirely from the heart, clearly describe a picture of what you will be doing once this issue is resolved or the goal is achieved and how incredible it is. Vividly convey in your recorded message the desired result of how things will turn out in a specific situation as you construct that narrative with your words. The feelings and emotions you relay in this type of recording are critical. They need to pack a mighty punch! Get ready to rock your own boat, and be determined to influence your mind to overcome every hurdle. To intensify the effect further, you can blast and repeat the recorded message throughout the day to flood your mind with the thoughts and behaviors you want to see in yourself.

    This free-flow approach is one I continue to use often, especially when I need a dose of courage or resolve. It also requires little preparation as I simply pick up my cell phone and hit record. I usually do a couple of versions to pick from, as my words pour out differently each time. From preparing for a stressful event to pushing hard through frustrating procrastination, this tactic positions me to run straight toward my giant and face it boldly.

    The bottom line is that whenever fear, anxiety, or overthinking starts to rise in me, my self-talk strategies fire up to dismantle it. I gather my thoughts and get my signature self-talk in motion to trigger the power and strength I need in order to press forward. I decide and record how I've determined it will be. Every message serves to refocus, refresh, and reinforce the *right* thoughts to keep my mind on track. I speak not only loud enough but specifically and often enough to override negativity before it can even take root. It's a matter of learning to be proactive and building confidence in my ability to take authority over my thoughts, one obstacle at a time. Without fail, the more I put my signature influence to work, the faster and more robust it becomes in effecting change.

Style 3: Interactive (To Speak Along With). This message style is remarkably engaging and commands your attention. You design a list of specific statements to say slowly and clearly, then repeat it a second time so you will be able to speak along with yourself as you listen to the recording. As you can imagine, this method amplifies the effect because you are simultaneously hearing your recorded and live voice. When you act in response to the recording, be sure to remain all-in as you talk with energy and passion. You can use this style to declare authoritative scriptures or boost your affirmations. It also promotes memorization as it engages you and moves you to respond. You drive the message deeper into your memory every time you hear and repeat the information.

Style 4: Study/Learning Technique. Using the 4-Step DARE System outlined in chapter 8, you can design signature recordings specifically for learning purposes. Before I even understood how to use my self-talk daily to influence my thought life, I used the sound of my recorded voice to study and learn important material. Years ago, I listened to cassette tape recordings I'd made to prepare for an important exam. Throughout the day, I played a simple recording of myself reading my notes and reviewing quiz questions, essentially talking to myself about the test. I listened again and again to absorb the information. Although the technology may have been different back then, the method proved valuable and highly effective. I credit it with helping me to maintain a high GPA. The lasting effect of each recording on my mind and memory was remarkable. Somehow, while taking the test, the recording surfaced inside me, with my voice clearly speaking the answers.

I continued to use my voice recordings as a profitable tool to study for tough licensing exams and other important purposes later in life. It became my "go-to" practice, and I found more and more ways to expand how I used my recorded voice to learn new things. Time after time, it proved to be a great asset to help me remember information and apply it to my life. Today I continue to use my 4-Step DARE System extensively to educate myself. Instead of allowing cherished details to slip away, I make self-talk recordings to help me retain relevant knowledge so I can continue to use it and benefit from it.

For example, I personalize and record key points or ideas from good books, articles, or other materials to create signature messages for myself. Sometimes I even repurpose them to use as affirmations or declarations. Instead of the valuable information being lost on a dusty bookshelf or buried in a file drawer, I keep it fresh and easily accessible. It allows me to keep learning, appreciating, and applying the gold nuggets to my life. It has become a great addition to my self-talk arsenal and improves my thinking. This simple practice creates a positive habit, increases my skills, and helps me *continue* putting the knowledge I'm gaining to work. And once again, I can listen anytime I hit the play button.

Life will never be the same when you give yourself the advantage of using your signature methods to educate, sharpen, and use your mind more powerfully. This simple process will help you study better and remember more. Based on making an audio recording of your own summarized notes and points from great books, training classes, videos, speeches, sermons, or articles, the knowledge you glean can live on and continue to impact your life in countless positive ways. With the wealth of knowledge God puts in our path, why not master how to keep putting the best ideas to work in your life?

RECORDING OPTIONS
Let's look at some specific options for *recording* your signature messages. A simple voice recorder app on your cell phone can keep your audio messages close and available for listening. Several recording apps are free and easy to learn, making it convenient to build your library of self-talk messages. You can also have the flexibility to transfer digital audio files onto other devices, including your tablet or computer. In either case, it's essential to have your messages clearly labeled or titled and accessible so you can reach for and use them on repeat. Also, I recommend you back up your recordings routinely to ensure they stay safe and protected.

ADDING BACKGROUND MUSIC: Although I have created most of my signature recordings with nothing more than the sound of my voice, I have designed some of my messages with background music. For example, I fall asleep to a relaxing health and wellness message I've created that contains soft music behind my voice. I've also enjoyed using a favorite motivational song behind the pep talks I make to use while exercising. It is an incredibly different experience to work out with my signature voice and message pumping into my mind.

Whenever you add background music to complement your signature recordings, be careful that it never overpowers or takes away from your voice's natural sound, clarity, or influence. It is often best to use primarily instrumental music on a low volume that is not too distracting. You can keep your recordings simple and basic or get highly creative in your arrangements to appeal to your tastes. Have fun with it, and make it your own. The priority is to keep your recording focused on your voice and the critical message you are relaying to your mind.

LISTENING OPTIONS
You can choose to listen to your signature self-talk messages actively or passively. Active listening is when you are *focused and intentional, not engaged in other activities at the same time.* Passive listening is listening as you are *in motion* or doing other things. Either way, keeping your signature messages playing loudly and fresh in your mind is the key to continuing the work of shaping your thinking. An *auto-replay* feature is also highly beneficial, allowing you to listen to your messages on a loop. Here are my recommendations regarding various listening options.

ACTIVE LISTENING: Dedicate daily time to sitting still in a relaxed state to focus on hearing and absorbing your voice and message. Savor the moments as you listen carefully and attentively. You can also create a specific routine to play your self-talk messages so your mind will get in the habit of expecting to listen. Picking a consistent time of day and a favorite place to sit can make the experience a familiar and inviting routine. Smiling can also be beneficial as it engages your brain and brings added pleasure to the listening process.

PASSIVE LISTENING: Whether driving, exercising, cleaning the house, or showering, you can take in your message without giving it your full attention. The auto-replay feature can be excellent for passive listening as it keeps repeating the message while you are involved in other tasks.

USING HEADPHONES: When listening to your audio recordings, whether actively or passively, I recommend using headphones in order to catch all the finely tuned nuances in your voice and make it an even more private experience. Not only do headphones reduce outside distractions, but the sound elements in your voice are more transparent and defined. They intensify the overall effect of *you* speaking directly to *you*. You can detect expression, energy, and emotion at a higher level. They let you pick up on recognizable emphasis on certain words, phrases, or points. Using headphones can draw you into listening at a deeper level, and it can improve how you connect with and receive the message.

ANCHORING, ASSOCIATING, AND ABSORBING: When you tie listening to your signature message with a specific activity, it can help to *anchor* it. For example, you can listen to a particular recording every time you do a routine daily task, like brushing your teeth or taking a walk. Before you know it, your mind will *associate* that particular message with doing that specific activity. You will begin to think automatically about that same message every time you show up to brush your teeth or start out the door for your walk. Learn to get creative in using the power of repetition to better *absorb* your signature self-talk. As you keep listening, find ways to plug your messages into your ordinary tasks and daily life to gain even more ground.

USING YOUR SENSES: We, indeed, are powerhouses within ourselves! God has given us extraordinary senses to create more extravagant and enjoyable life experiences. Every time you engage more of yourself in the listening process, you will associate listening to your signature message with the feeling of great pleasure. Have fun experimenting with involving more of your senses. You can watch the sunrise, light a candle, sip hot coffee, or snuggle up in your favorite cozy blanket. Your senses of sight, smell, taste, touch, and hearing can all help to energize the process. Get your dopamine flowing as you use one, a combination, or all of your senses to intensify the effect of listening to your signature self-talk.

As you can see, there are endless possibilities you can attach to listening to your signature recordings. These simple connections can enhance the experience and make it more intense, pleasurable, and deeply ingrained. You can build unique preferences into your routine and look forward to how you uplift, influence, and encourage yourself every day. Whether sitting still or on the go, the key is to keep listening and planting the seeds of your signature pieces to create the mindset, habits, and life you want. Believe that things are taking root and you are making progress, even if you don't see it immediately. Trust that God is continuing to work powerfully on your behalf.

Enjoy the signature recordings you create. Make listening time a particularly captivating part of your day and life. Remain consistent and committed to your listening schedule to keep moving closer to your desired results. Stay engaged and keep your influential voice and messages playing loudly in your heart and mind. You will feel alive, healthier, and more hopeful whenever you *hear* your signature self-talk messages and *feel* them stirring your faith into action.

**Use your signature self-talk to stir the gift,
fan the flame, and ignite the fire!**

DAILY APPLICATIONS AND STRATEGIES
Developing your daily practices to influence your thinking and actions can change your confidence level and approach to life. Engaging in a persistent, healthy mindset gives you an empowering edge! Dare to incorporate the following strategies daily to help you gain clarity, sharpen your mind, and strengthen your resolve as you move toward your goals.

FRAMING YOUR DAY: The beauty of audio recordings is that they are convenient and easy to incorporate into your everyday life, morning, noon, or night. However, it is worth noting that the most pivotal moments in your day are when you first wake up and *enter* consciousness and just before you close your eyes to *leave* consciousness. These brief moments profoundly impact you. Why not start using them to your full benefit? Your thoughts upon awakening can set the tone for the entire day ahead. Likewise, the reflections you experience as you close your eyes at night can affect your sleep quality and dreams. Using your signature self-talk to take full advantage of these precious windows of time can be empowering.

Here is how to take the reins in what I refer to as *framing your day*. Create and record a short signature piece to play as soon as you wake up and before you close your eyes at night. You decide what will positively frame your day, whether it involves a special prayer, scripture, affirmation, or gratitude statement. This is a perfect way to get in the habit of having your voice influence your mind as you intentionally guide your thoughts to start and finish each day. Simple yet packed with intention and purpose, framing your day with recorded messages will help to build your thought muscle rapidly. With your eloquent message ready to roll every morning and every night, all you have to do is hit play. You can change the message anytime and try new ideas to keep it stimulating and keep you engaged and growing.

GOAL ACHIEVEMENT STRATEGY: Creating a signature audio recording of your personal or professional goals could be one of the best-kept secrets you will ever learn. Day by day, your own voice will lead the way in transforming your career, business, and life. As we've already touched on, your personal recording can effectively keep your life goals in front of you daily. The ease of repetition and consistency is unmatched. Even more, as you continue to play your same goal-blueprint message and implant it into your thinking each day, it will absorb deeper and deeper into your mind and memory.

Consider how adding a simple audio recording with a clear outline of your goals could increase your chance of achievement. Incredibly, as you take this one extra step to listen to and reinforce your aspirations, you will join the elite few who faithfully review their goals daily. Continual exposure is key to ensuring that your pursuits stay top of mind. Your recordings can raise the bar on keeping your goals alive and activated in your mind.

What you focus on with intention and emotion can ignite your thinking, speed up results, and move you toward your desired success.

Big messages can fit in small moments, and extraordinary transformations can happen on ordinary days.

SELF-GUIDED VISUALIZATION: Your God-given imagination is a dynamic tool to develop and use for building a more vibrant and meaningful life. Visualization is simply using your imagination to form a mental picture of something. It allows you to see beyond current circumstances and explore where you want to go. You can move past any limit to a better place in your imagination. You create the image in your mind. Visualization brings color and hope into your soul. It is truly a magnificent treasure God placed inside each one of us.

The benefit of using your imagination to visualize what you want to achieve is stunning. From brainstorming ideas to exploring your personal goals, dreams, an exciting event, or a business plan, you must know how to use the gift of your imagination to produce wondrous things in your life. It will grow when you intentionally engage your imagination in some small way daily. With focus, practice, and repetition, your visualizations can be very effective in your success journey. What you produce in your imagination *today* can change your life *tomorrow* and, as a result, many other lives along the way. It's time to take possession of the dreams God dropped in your heart and start mapping out the details and creating them with your imagination.

One of the most rewarding ways you can use your signature self-talk is by creating self-guided visualizations. When you design your signature message to walk you through a self-guided visualization, your influential voice can help you develop your vision more easily and clearly. If it's challenging to get your imagination in gear or get a clear picture, put the ultimate guide to work to help you engage. That guide is *you*. Your heart and mind know better than anyone where you want to go and how you want your future to look. Write it out, make it clear, record it, and then relax as you allow your trusted voice to lead the way.

When your signature recording guides you through the personal details of your vision, you will not only see it in your mind but also hear it in your voice! Outline every aspect of driving your dream car. Explain your day in the bookstore signing your best-selling novel. As you listen and resonate with your words and emotion, it will be easier to feel what your voice is describing to you. When you've brilliantly painted a picture and aligned your thoughts to create a vivid experience, you will get your mind excited about seeing and accomplishing it. With each repetition, you are actively sparking more clarity, courage, and desire to fulfill the ambition or goal. You are providing the fuel your heart, mind, and soul need to keep moving you closer and closer to the dream becoming a reality. Every time you listen to your self-guided visualization recording, it is a journey toward your imagined finished goal and ultimate success.

SCHEDULING OPTIONS

Set yourself up for success *daily*! Make it a habit to reach for the signature messages you've prepared. For a specific outcome, listen to the *same* signature message at least three times throughout the day for thirty days or until you reach your breakthrough. If you want an even more intense effect, dial up the repetition. For general-purpose self-talk recordings, such as daily declarations or encouraging words to minister to *yourself*, listen to your messages on an ongoing basis to boost self-motivation and strengthen your mind and spirit.

We can't forget about one more critical element of our self-talk arsenal that needs to be loaded and ready to go: the signature recordings we create for use on an urgent or as-needed basis. One of the top self-talk recordings I use to arm myself is a "battle plan" I designed. When an emotional storm or spiritual attack hits, I lead myself, step by step, through a clear action plan to take control so I can rise up and stand firm in my God-given authority. I've planned, prepared, and recorded the *right* thoughts to saturate my mind during a tough battle. When we fight the *right* way with the *right* weapons, we can prevail against any enemy.

Whatever mission we need our signature self-talk messages to help us accomplish, they can help us stay armed and prepared. Establishing a habit of listening to our best voice is paramount as it instills direction, encouragement, and high-quality thoughts into our souls. Every listening experience will quicken our minds to move us faster and further toward the intended outcome we seek.

USING A TRACKING SHEET: Remember to track and measure your progress as you listen to your signature recordings. You can log your self-talk messages on a simple spreadsheet you design and create. Always have a master list to include all of your signature recordings. You can include the date you started, the topic, and the length of each recorded message. Make sure to clearly label, title, or number the signature messages stored on your recording device so you can find them quickly and easily. You can also prioritize messages by keeping a top-five list so you can go straight to the favorites in your current playlist. You can listen to them one at a time or line up a series to play daily.

Your spreadsheet log will keep you on track with a clear picture of the topics you are working on achieving. Set a clear and specific goal for your daily number of listening repetitions. Just as significant, have an area on your tracking sheet to note your results, breakthroughs, and answered prayers. Remember, elevating and celebrating are mega important for growing and moving forward. Have fun seeing the new patterns develop and your life-changing progress unfold.

SETTING REMINDERS: Commit to a schedule and set alarms or reminders when you have a solid plan for listening to your signature messages. The more you hear and think about them, the more dominating they will become in your mind and the more they will produce in your life. Like a magnet, you will keep moving toward your most intent thoughts. Keep building positive new pathways and implanting your signature messages into long-term memory. "Let God transform you into a new person by changing the way you *think*. Then you will learn to know God's will for you, which is good and pleasing and perfect" (Romans 12:2 NLT, italics mine).

MASTERING YOUR THOUGHT LIFE
Whenever you hit the play button on your recordings with the desire to learn, grow, strengthen your thought life, or embolden your faith, you are mastering your own mind. Your signature self-talk provides the means to build your arsenal of personal, practical, profound messaging that will help you stay attentive to your thought life. Dare to develop a wealth of self-talk recordings to rotate through that will keep you moving forward. Continually put good things in your mind. Decide what you want to *dominate* your focus and determine the *right* messages to keep on repeat at the *right* time. Know your go-to recordings to play daily or whenever you need a reset or pick-me-up. Your messages can be updated at any time or retired at any point. They can be used short-term or long-term or added to a treasured lifelong collection (which we will discuss more in the next chapter). These are *the* life-shaping creations you have designed to help you be all you want to be and all that God created you to be.

> **"Spend your time and energy in the exercise of keeping spiritually fit."**
> **—1 Timothy 4:7 TLB**

With minimal time and effort invested, your signature recordings can continue to pay rich dividends. You can learn to create captivating self-talk messages that will help you live a life you absolutely love. Whether standing up to fear and anxiety or advancing your highest ambitions, you are putting your faith into mighty action as you talk to, influence, and encourage yourself to live your best life. What you tackle, you can conquer. As I have become my own expert self-talk strategist, you will too! Most of all, make it a regular, natural practice to stir up your God-given gifts every day and use them fiercely in your life and in the world.

How can we find *true* success in life and keep expanding our influence? Let's talk about it in the next chapter.

Chapter 10

TRUE SUCCESS AND
A LASTING LEGACY

In a story once told by Earl Nightingale, a brilliant motivational speaker, he shared an interesting perspective on *success*. He explained how a famous restaurateur was being interviewed by a reporter who asked, "*When* did you become successful?" and he replied, "I was successful when I was sleeping on park benches. Because I *knew* what I wanted to do and that I would do it."[15] What a remarkable testimony of a man being able to influence and encourage *himself* beyond his circumstances and toward his eventual success.

Have you ever thought about what *true* success looks like for you? I understand that the world typically looks for evidence of success on the outside. But we have to wonder, when does success really begin? In the seen or the unseen? Can unlocking our unseen God-given treasures inside be the key to unlocking our success *outside*? What can happen when we truly take possession of and begin to use the faith, strength, power, and endless resources God has entrusted to us? Will it cause our success in life to begin the inevitable shift from the impossible over to the possible? Most importantly, if we don't experience success *inside* first, will we ever be able to experience true success in whatever we achieve or accumulate in the world?

Whether today you are a CEO leading a company or sleeping on a park bench, there's more to your story. Regardless of how your outer circumstances may appear, it's about having deep faith and a God-sized perspective below the surface on the inside. As we can see from the success-minded businessman in the story, what really counts is how you *think* every day and how you talk to and influence *yourself*.

STIR UP THE GIFT WITHIN YOU

Your life is on a new trajectory, and your signature self-talk will be the resounding catalyst for change. Every time you actively stir up your gifts, you can draw, define, and brighten the vision of your successful future ahead. Sometimes dreams feel so close. Other times, so far away. But you are the only one who can keep stirring them up and pulling them closer. You must keep *seeing* them, *feeling* them, and *believing* in them if you want to close the gap. Imagine how continually having your burning desire fired up and pumping through you will help you stay engaged and move forward. Don't look back and wonder how your life could have been different. Stay committed and *keep talking yourself* toward your intrinsic God-given destiny. Today is the day to start taking action on the breakthroughs you need!

Below is a simple self-talk *starter* you can record to get the ball rolling. Rally your passion, grab your device, and go for it! Then play it on a loop three times to get used to hearing and feeling your signature voice, authority, message, and the emotion behind it.

Today, there is nothing, absolutely nothing, that can happen that God and I together can't handle! I can manage whatever life brings. I am faithful, reliable, capable, and dependable. Whatever happens, He will make a way! I stand firm no matter where I am, what I'm going through, or how it looks or feels. I am filled, overflowing, and on fire as I continually stir up and use the strength and power of God inside me every day. I don't just survive; I thrive! I put my faith into action, and I stay focused on what builds me up and strengthens me. I think it, speak it, remember it, and live it. I keep it playing loudly in my heart and in my mind. No matter what, I stay passionate about influencing, encouraging, and motivating myself. I stand tall and well-equipped today, tomorrow, and forever. This is who I am and who God created me to be. My faith and courage were built for this!

As you gain traction in becoming your own personal self-talk *advocate,* your mind may start to flag the times you speak ill of yourself. What may have been overlooked on prior occasions now stands out and begins to *feel* different. For example, if you casually say, "I'm always so clumsy," or "I am so terrible at remembering names," your self-bashing statements now seem to strike a sour chord. They clash with what you have been actively telling your heart and mind in your recordings. Before you know it, you start to block negativity and critical thoughts and turn them around faster and more easily than ever before. Your signature self-talk work has shifted your patterns, beliefs, and thought *environment*. You've raised the bar in training your mind to expect better quality thinking and a higher level of self-talk. Gradually, your entire thought life becomes a place where you thrive in your view of yourself and the world. You will be so well practiced at finding the *best* in who you are that it will soon become an automatic response.

Whatever happens in your world, your inner force can remain steady. It will soon become natural to stand up and consistently believe in yourself. I cannot tell you the countless times that the stronger me has shown up to encourage the weaker me. God revealed to me how to use my own voice to minister to the deepest parts of my inner world and to cheer me on every day. Although I always appreciated any outer support that existed around me, somehow it could never compare with my internal support system and God's powerful gifts at work inside me. The world could sometimes fail me, but there is great comfort in knowing that God never has and never will.

As we know, faith comes by *hearing*! Like a muscle, your hearing will assist you in deciphering your signature influence and experiencing how it can build you up. Your self-talk will become more defined and evident the more you use it. It will grow and expand into new insights you can explore about yourself, your thinking, and your relationship with God. When you learn how to *maximize* your inner world, you will realize how directly it affects and actually *creates* your outer world.

I dare you to fire up and begin using your radiant gifts to make your visions clearer and more prominent. As you structure your ideas and fine-tune your signature self-talk system, it can propel you into new beginnings. Be obsessed with what you put in your mind and spirit daily. When you do, you are on your way to creating some serious momentum and building a bigger, better, more vibrant life.

BUILDING AND LEAVING A LASTING LEGACY

As we've seen in every step of this journey, talking to God leads the way to learning how to speak to *ourselves* with more influence and authority. As a result, our robust self-talk leads us to impact the world around us more profoundly. Finally, it can build a lasting legacy. As you develop and master your signature gifts, your life becomes a model that can help others understand how to live their *thought lives* by design as well. You can become a *torchbearer* who inspires others to stir up their signature gifts and raise their self-talk to new levels.

In our lifetime, we have the opportunity to influence ourselves and others as well as history. The things we do *now* can continue to have a multiplying effect over generations. Even more, what we do in everyday life is absorbed by our children, whether young or grown, from our habits and behaviors to family traditions and how we handle life at every turn. Good or bad, our life makes a distinct and lasting impression.

Is it any wonder that our world cares earnestly about memorializing people, places, and historical events? Big or small, tangible ways of formalizing meaningful memories are created. They are meant to etch the importance in people's hearts and minds and mark history. Each remembrance established, even an action as simple as building a pile of rocks, is set apart to serve a worthy purpose. What do these efforts accomplish? Marking miracles, highlighting victories, or even flagging painful lessons never to be repeated can help bolster faith for the future and build up the strength of those coming behind us.

Imagine what could be accomplished if you were willing to share the lessons that have profoundly shaped your life. What if your life experiences could help your loved ones stand firm and prevail in their own tough times? The wealth of knowledge from your mountains and valleys, victories and defeats, can provide valuable wisdom and encouragement. Above all, you can help your loved ones achieve a strong sense of identity as they learn to influence and encourage *themselves* to live their best lives every day.

DON'T JUST LIVE LIFE WELL; LEAVE IT WELL
My burning desire for you in writing this book is that you would *live* life well today and also create a legacy that will help you one day *leave* this life well. Consider what you have gained from those who are no longer here. Some you had the joy of knowing. Others in your family line contributed to your life in ways you will never know. Either way, guidance from those we love, respect, and trust the most can be deeply significant.

Imagine if previous generations had the technology that we have available to us today. What if you could hear the voice of your great-great-grandmother or grandfather sharing a special life-lifting message on an audio recording? (Remember the incredible virtues of voice-only communication mentioned in chapter 7). What would it be like to listen to their sincerity, laughter, and unique thoughts about life? When heartfelt expressions are captured in an audible message, they can live on and continue to make a worthwhile impact.

Several years ago, I lost my parents, seven weeks apart. As many others have experienced, there was a great sense of loss in not being able to hear their voices anymore. What I had often taken for granted over the years was now gone. I found myself going back through every old recorded message I could find so I could listen to their voices. One of the treasures I came across was a voicemail of Dad and Mom giggling as they chimed in to sing me an out-of-tune rendition of "Happy Birthday." Now, I pull up that audio recording yearly and have my dear parents sing to me on my birthday. As simple as it is, it means everything to me.

Regardless of where we may be today or tomorrow, God can still use and speak through our lives. Think about all the words and sentiments preserved and passed forward over centuries in books, letters, recordings, art, music, and more. Every life experience is significant and valuable, including yours. We can never underestimate how God, at any time, may touch another life with *our* life stories, lessons, and experiences.

CURATING A SELF-TALK COLLECTION
I encourage you to curate your signature library, piece by piece and year by year, to develop a collection that will outlive you one day. As you build on it and create a heartfelt masterpiece, it can be shared and drawn upon for generations. As short or long as it may be, your recorded audio messages can continue to plant seeds in the

hearts, minds, and lives of your loved ones and become a rich part of your *legacy*. As we covered in chapter 7, the *voice-only* experience is remarkable and unique. Without visual distraction, the focus on hearing your sound, tone, words, expressions, and emotions can be intensified. Your voice can comfort, inspire, and reveal more than you recognize.

It's important to realize that your life is significant to this generation and to future generations as well. Be generous in extending a loving touch or sharing your stories and life experiences. Don't just settle to take your place in *past* history. Take hold of the opportunity to have a place in affecting *future* history. Are you willing to help strengthen the faith and lives of those you love who will live on after you?

Just like creating a "greatest hits" collection, let me share a few ideas for using your signature messages to build a unique legacy for your loved ones:

1. Set up a designated digital folder for all the legacy recordings you want to collect. Create a list and keep it updated with each message you want to share, either now or in the future.

2. At the end of each year, or anytime you feel inspired, record your highlights or most meaningful experiences and the valuable lessons you learned from them. Talk about the struggles you've walked through and the courage and wisdom you gained. It is a great act of love to share your stories of faith and what God has done in your life. Your voice, words, warmth, and expressions carry the essence of you and will make the messages come alive! What you impart will enrich and help those listening navigate their lives in a better way.

3. Take some time to record an outline of the spiritual beliefs, family values, traditions, and work ethic you've chosen to live by and what all these mean to you. Share your wit, personality, and humor as you describe your failures and successes and what helped you to handle them. Think of the confident and fighting spirit you can instill and encourage in your loved ones. Your messages can contribute to bringing comfort and transforming the lives of others more than you could ever imagine.

4. Another idea is to make individual audio messages for special people in your life. What you could write on paper will never be able to accomplish what the sound of your loving voice can convey and do. An individual sentiment that you personally prepare and speak from the heart in your voice is an irreplaceable and priceless gift.

5. If you prefer, involve a family member or friend to help set up an interview-style message to record. Questions or topics can be prepared in advance, or a conversation can merely unfold. Have fun with it! Get creative in communicating what you want to pass on and make it meaningful.

Like throwing a rock into a still pond, your legacy messages can ripple out to the world and be used to contribute to other people and generations. The fire that burns in your signature sound, spirit, and faith can be a guiding light and a lasting influence. What you share could make a genuine difference in how others think, solve problems, and live their lives. Putting your treasured messages in tangible form to be passed forward opens up a world of possibilities. But it can only happen if you take the steps to do it. What words and ideas has

God given *you* to bring support and solutions to the next generation?

Every one of us has the opportunity to begin shaping our legacy, starting with positively influencing our own lives and self-talk. Live your life *now* in a way that will cause people to want to hear what you have to say *later*. Just like in the parable of the talents in Matthew 25:14–30, God expects us to be faithful, competent, and willing to take risks in order to invest and multiply the valuable things we have been given. This includes our gifts, talents, voice, and life experiences. It can be a terrible waste to play it too safe or to bury them. It's never too soon to start building what will one day be a lasting legacy.

Before we conclude, take a moment to reflect on how each chapter has been priming and equipping you to be more influential and transformative in your own life. With that in mind, it's time to step out in faith and into the SELF-TALK DARE!

Conclusion

THE SELF-TALK DARE

We began this great adventure by setting out to build a strong, stable house on three solid pillars that could produce a bountiful life. We were awakened to realize how our quality of life can hinge on how we talk to God, ourselves, and others. We zoomed in to discover the magnitude of our signature self-talk and God-given influence and authority. We gained a new perspective on how our inner gifts—including our abilities, courage, confidence, perseverance, and more—in God's strength and power, could progress from a tiny spark to a flame to the beacon of light that our lives can become. As we opened our minds to learning the 4-Step DARE System for designing our daily thoughts, we grasped how our self-talk can ultimately influence our life and destiny. We began to see and understand *how* God, from start to finish, uses each of us to effectively talk to, influence, and encourage *ourselves.*

As you can see, this book takes you outside the box of typical thinking regarding self-talk. There is an intentional focus on *preventing* unhealthy self-talk versus overcoming it. The concepts challenge you to move beyond the standard practice of self-discipline and into the broader authority you have to *influence yourself.* The game plan emphasizes staying in a position of *offense* over defense. Each of these principles has a specific purpose in helping you to master the art of influencing yourself.

I hope you can now understand that developing your signature self-talk is one of the most important investments you will ever make in yourself and your future. Once you learn to live from the inside out, it's an exciting journey to discover more about who you are and who God designed you to be. Your inner world can come alive, and your life can soar as you learn to fan the flame and ignite many God-given gifts waiting to be used.

Now, *I dare you* to put the techniques you've learned into practice every day to keep your house rock-solid, thriving, and ready for any storm. When you cultivate your own signature self-talk, it will help you stand firm and dominate in the battles of faith over fear. Your life will be transformed when you stay committed to preserving an unshakable internal support system. Be strategic in your tactics and unwavering in holding a winning belief system. *Stay* on the offensive as you continue to use your God-given authority over your thinking and life. Make it a high priority to develop a lifestyle of positively influencing and encouraging yourself every single day.

I dare you to be passionate about taking possession of and embracing your personal success in the unseen, where it all begins. Stay consistent in visualizing it, believing it, expecting it, and preparing for it! Continually put your faith into specific action with the 4-Step DARE System to be ready to do your part. A shift from the impossible to the possible is some of God's best work in your life, but He must have the cooperation of your *thinking*. This season, it's time to move what has been waiting in the seemingly impossible column over to the possible column. It begins with the decision to agree, believe, and take hold of what you are producing in your thought life.

Your mouth is a gold mine right under your nose. The precious instrument to slay giants and speak life to your soul. It expresses your thoughts, feelings, and ideas. Its incomparable influence can help you reach for life in all of its fullness. It's time to mine that gold and *extract* the precious treasures you can put work in your life. When you step into your signature role and wholeheartedly develop your God-given power and authority in speaking to yourself, watch how it amplifies your voice and your presence in the world.

As you *dare* to put these life-changing principles into play *behind closed doors*, your success will expand and flow from private to public. The more you elevate your life, the more outstanding achievements you will have to celebrate. Today is the day to take command in how you will lead yourself forward and step into living God's wildly abundant life for you!

ACCEPTING THE DARE

If you are ready to step boldly into becoming the designer, creator, and controller of your own signature self-talk and thought life, all that's left is to make it official. I invite you to accept this *Self-Talk Dare* by doing the following:

1. Seize this moment and turn off every noise or distraction around you. Get to a quiet place where

SIGNATURE SELF-TALK

you can be alone, silent, and still before God. Let your heart intently seek Him, and then stop and listen. Ask Him to fill you with His best gifts and to help you in your journey to continually stir up and use them from this day forward.
2. Write your signature below to commit that you are all-in to create and use your signature self-talk in full force in order to revolutionize and transform your thinking and life. Then mark this important date on your calendar.
3. To memorialize this game-changing milestone, take a minute to make a quick audio recording with the date and time. Express your sincere excitement and commitment to accept this Self-Talk Dare and start the adventure of speaking confidently into your own life and *influencing yourself* with your own, one-of-a-kind, signature self-talk!

_____   _____

YOUR SIGNATURE   DATE

Congratulations on taking this monumental step. But the journey doesn't end here. As you get out there and show yourself what you're made of, connect with us online for additional support, training, and resources to help you build and *keep* your self-talk arsenal strong. Join us in this *self-talk movement* to ignite a stronger thought life! Visit us at www.selftalkmovement.com.

NOTES

1. See the video capturing this experiment at "Ten Meter Tower | NYT Op-Docs," *The New York Times*, YouTube video, January 17, 2018, https://www.youtube.com/watch?v=5QMlIjSnt_E.
2. For the full story, go to "Randy Phillips and the Incredible Story Behind Danny Gokey's song 'Tell Your Heart to Beat Again,'" KeepTheFaith.com, YouTube video, April 28, 2016, https://www.youtube.com/watch?v=FYbVQfuBd7s.
3. "Life Expectancy in the U.S. Declined a Year and Half in 2020," National Center for Health Statistics (NCHS), Center for Disease Control and Protection, CDC.gov, July 21, 2021, https://www.cdc.gov/nchs/pressroom/nchs_press_releases/2021/202107.htm#print.
4. Rachel Gillett, "How Walt Disney, Oprah Winfrey, and 19 Other Successful People Rebounded After Getting Fired," Inc.com, October 7, 2015, https://www.inc.com/xintian-tina-wang/lorenzo-lewis-confess-project-barbers-mental-health.html.
5. Bronnie Ware, *Top Five Regrets of the Dying: A Life Transformed by the Dearly Departing* (Carlsbad, CA: Hay House, 2019), 37.
6. Bronnie Ware, *Top Five Regrets of the Dying*, 102.
7. Shiho Fukada, "Japan's Prisons Are a Haven for Elderly Women," *Bloomberg Businessweek*, March 16, 2018, https://www.bloomberg.com/news/features/2018-03-16/japan-s-prisons-are-a-haven-for-elderly-women?leadSource=uverify%20wall.

8   Luke Mahoney, "The Rise of Companion Robots in Japan," JapanToday.com, December 23, 2019, https://japantoday.com/category/tech/the-rise-of-companion-robots-in-japan.
9   "Loneliness and the Workplace," Cigna.com, 2020 report, accessed December 16, 2022, https://www.cigna.com/static/www-cigna-com/docs/about-us/newsroom/studies-and-reports/combatting-loneliness/cigna-2020-loneliness-factsheet.pdf.
10 Brett Archibald, *Alone: Lost Overboard in the Indian Ocean* (New York: Thomas Dunne Books, 2017).
11 Gerardo Riquelme, "Ruth Beitia Wins Historic High Jump Gold," adapted by Sarah Farrell, Marca.com, updated August 21, 2016, https://www.marca.com/en/olympic-games/2016/08/21/57b9730b46163fe8328b45f2.html.
12 Michael W. Kraus, "Voice-Only Communication Enhances Empathic Accuracy," *The American Psychologist*, 72, no. 7 (Oct. 2017): 644–54, https://doi.org/10.1037/amp0000147.
13 Jean-Julien Aucouturier, Petter Johansson, Lars Hall, Rodrigo, Segnini, Lolita Mercadié, and Katsumi Watanabe, "Covert Digital Manipulation of Vocal Emotion Alter Speakers' Emotional States in a Congruent Direction," *Proceedings of the National Academy of Sciences of the United States of America* 113, no. 4 (January 2016): 948-53, https://doi.org/10.1073/pnas.1506552113.
14 Jean-Julien Aucouturier et al.
15 Earl Nightingale, 1957 spoken word recording *How To Lead the Field In The Modern World* series, part one (of twelve) titled *The Magic Word-Attitude* published by Nightingale-Conant Corporation, YouTube video, coachAOG, January 10, 2016, https://www.youtube.com/watch?v=AZxV7tZyJDc.

www.ingramcontent.com/pod-product-compliance
Lightning Source LLC
Chambersburg PA
CBHW020338010526
44119CB00035B/446/J